I wonder
how the shepherds felt
that very special night?
Or the wise men
who were following
a star so big and bright?
I wonder
if they knew the gift
this tiny Child would bring?
For the moment
Jesus Christ was born,
God gave us everything!

Twelve Things
I Want My Kids
To Remember
FOREVER

Twelve Things I Want My Kids To Remember

FOREVER

JERRY B. JENKINS

MOODY PRESS

CHICAGO

©1991 by
JERRY B. JENKINS

ISBN: 0-8024-8756-4

1 2 3 4 5 6 Printing/BC/Year 95 94 93 92 91

Printed in the United States of America

To Dallas, Chad, and Michael

CONTENTS

Among other books by Jerry Jenkins:

Non-Fiction
Lessons Learned Early
Hymns For Personal Devotions
Rekindled (with Pat and Jill Williams)
Hedges: Loving Your Marriage Enough to Protect It

Biography
Out of the Blue (with Orel Hershiser)
Meadowlark (with Meadowlark Lemon)
Carry Me (with Christine Wyrtzen)
The Luis Palau Story
Sweetness (with Walter Payton)
Bad Henry (with Hank Aaron)
God's Love in Action (with Sammy Tippit)

Adult Fiction
Rookie
The Operative
The Margo Mysteries
The Jennifer Grey Mysteries

Children's Fiction
Dallas O'Neil and the Baker Street Sports Club
The Dallas O'Neil Mysteries
The Bradford Family Adventures
The Tara Chadwick Series

A NOTE TO YOU

T hough this book was truly written for and to my own kids, my hope is that you might benefit from it. Whether you have your own children or grandchildren, or perhaps have no children or aren't even married, feel free to read over my shoulder as I attempt to remind my kids of a dozen broad issues I want them never to forget.

The day may come when you'll want to formulate your own truths on paper—maybe not in a book, but simply in a list—to make certain someone knows clearly some of your own philosophies of life.

Your truths may in no way resemble mine. You may have just one or two, or twenty. Regardless, it's the communicating of them that is important. My hope is that this book might serve as a tool to aid you in communicating truth with a capital T at the level of the child in your life.

The rest of this book may be viewed as private communication, permission for the revealing of which I have received from my kids.

I hope it's of some help or encouragement or, at least, entertainment to you.

JERRY B. JENKINS

INTRODUCTION

Guys, you have to know how much I love you. Then again, maybe you don't. Of course you don't. I couldn't fathom my parents' love until I was grown and gone and had kids of my own. It's taken me twenty years of married life and watching your tireless mother to realize a fraction of what my mother did for me every day.

The same is true for all the ways my father showed his love, but there is something unique about the daily, nitty-gritty of a mother's love. More about that later.

I realize I am an archetypical, obnoxious father, naming our little homestead after you guys (Three Son Acres) and mounting poster-sized photos of you on my den wall.

I talk about you endlessly to anyone who'll listen—and too often to anyone who even pretends to listen.

I've risked cheapening the very meaning of words that should mean everything when I tell you several times a day that I love you. Sometimes you respond, "I know, Dad," and I say, "You want me to quit telling you?" and you say, "No, it's all right."

I've seen too many parents who don't back up their verbal expressions of love, and I don't want to be numbered among them. I want to prove it every day, not by spoiling you or by having our entire home life revolve around you, but by so ordering my priorities that you know what you mean to me.

That means not shutting you out while I'm working, when I've told you and told you that you mean more to me than my work. That means making it to your activities, sometimes at the expense of my own (I sure hate to miss those boring meetings!).

Your time with us has already flown by so quickly that we've come to believe those predictions our elders made—and which we thought so silly—when you were born: "It'll seem like a week, and they'll be off to college." So, those drives to school, to church, to soccer, baseball, and basketball games are for only a short time.

Oh, let's get serious. When you're gone I'll miss those the most. Combine my love of sports with the thrill of seeing my own kids play, and you get one of the most fun things I do. It's no sacrifice. I can't get enough of it.

Being raised as you have been—and as we were—by born-again, evangelical, fundamental, independent, pro-life conservatives has its advantages and its drawbacks. Until you become adults and start looking at life through your hearts instead of your heads, you may think that more things in this world are black and white than is really the case.

I could fill a book like this with twelve things from the Bible alone that I want you to remember forever, but given how and where you were raised, and the churches and schools you have attended, you'll likely remember the doctrinal basics whether you want to or not. Our prayer is that you will know the important, unchanging truth because it was modeled for you (albeit imperfectly) and because it has been proved in your lives as much as it was taught, lectured, preached, or driven into you.

The older I get and the more complex life seems to me, the simpler the great truths become. I've met and read and sat under and been privileged to be influenced by many great thinkers. But when you really get down to it, the only things that really matter are that God loves you, God cares about you, Jesus died for your sins, Jesus is alive, and Jesus is coming again.

I know there are theologies and doctrines and shades of meaning and denominational differences and distinctives. I am also aware that if I were more of an intellect perhaps some of those issues might seem as important to me as the five I listed above. But if you live your lives according to those truths—supplemented by a bedrock belief in the truth and authority of Scripture—you will find yourself loving and living for others, eager to see them come to Christ. You will find yourself going to church even when no one is making you, missions-minded even when it's not the most convenient, serving when you'd rather be served.

Oh, there are many more than a dozen things I really want you to remember forever. The majority of those I hope have been seared into your minds. It seems we tell you, remind you, cajole, encourage, crab, and nag every day some thousand things we imply you should already know.

So when I think about those things I want to be sure you remember when you're out from under our roof, I have to choose carefully. I think about those things that are not so obvious, that you have not been bombarded with at home, church, and school. I've made these points, or tried to, all along the way, but I want to record them here in case they were missed.

Some will cause you to roll your eyes and say, "Dad, how could we have missed that one?" Others you will squint at and say, "Really? I never knew you felt that way."

There will be those who criticize these for being too ordinary, too earthy, not spiritual enough. As I say, I hope the spiritual is embedded in you by now. And the only reason I make this private discourse public is that it might encourage others to document what they feel is most important. My twelve things will appear trivial to some, baffling to others. I might not find an overlapping truth in three other parents' lists of unforgettable axioms.

That's OK. These are for you.

You know how much I love you.

Well, at least you know *that* I love you.

Someday you'll know how much.

Only by then I'll love you more.

My life's goal is to stay ahead of your knowledge. I always want to love you more than you can know.

Love, Dad

LOVE
IS
AS
LOVE
DOES

1

LOVE IS AS LOVE DOES

If you haven't already, some day you will fall in love. Being "in love" is a misnomer, a meaningless, heart-thumping rush that's fun while it lasts, and it is so profound that no one will be able to talk you out of it. You will read these pages and know in advance that crushes, infatuation, and puppy love are tricks of the mind and heart, but when it happens to you, it will be different. No one has ever loved anyone the way I love her, you'll say. This is bigger, more cosmic, more real, spiritual, dramatic, deep. In truth your feelings may be based on more than just looks or even personality. You may fall in love with someone's mind, her way of expressing herself, her body language.

It'll pass. It always does.

But when you're in the throes of it, you will not be dissuaded. This is eternal, you'll say. This is more real to me than my relationship with God.

I remember well the first time I fell in love. I was ripe for it. It was the summer before my junior year in high school. I had had girl friends, someone to walk to class or talk to on the phone till my parents threatened to bill me. But I had not been in love.

A family moved to town, and somehow I was enlisted to help them move in. Their daughter, who just had to be in college, was a leggy, fresh-faced, quick-smiling girl who loved to talk and listen and looked you right in the eye, especially if she thought you were in college too. It emerged that we were the same age.

Fifteen. She would be a high school classmate.

The first time we shared a ride home from a church activity and held hands, I was smitten. What a boon to self-confidence! A girl everyone could see was a knockout was "going" with me! For days I could think of nothing or no one else. I doodled her name, found reasons to call her, wrote her notes, hung around with her.

The night we'd sat holding hands in the car for all of six or seven minutes was heavenly. That was better than any athletic success I'd ever had!

I was in love. How could anything be more beautiful, more perfect?

For me it was fun while it lasted and remains a harmless memory. But here's the problem with my all-too-common story and the truth I'd like you to remember: *being in love* is not love.

Love is not a feeling or even a state of being. Cold and unromantic as this may sound, I am not "in love" with your mother. I love her. It's an act of the will. It's something I do.

Though people who don't know us may read that and think I've saddled myself with a burdensome assignment, you know better. You remark on how your mom and I seem to really like each other, talk to each other, touch each other, flirt with each other, show affection to each other. Yes, ours is a love relationship, but the love is a verb, not a noun.

That first time I fell in love, what or whom was I in love with? I thought I loved the girl. I didn't know the girl! She looked great, and she smiled a lot. I don't even know whether I liked what she said as much as that she said it to me. I was in love with being in love. It felt great to be the object of someone else's attention, especially someone who was impressive to others. It did wonders for my ego. I confess that even today I like being married to a woman others think is wonderful and beautiful. And she is. But that is not the basis for love as a verb.

What I discovered about my first "love" was that she had a more serious boyfriend back where she came from. He was older. He drove. In fact, he had a job, money, his own car. I was a diversion to her, a nice guy who flattered her. When my sensibilities were rocked by this vision of loveliness using me, it was almost too much for a teenager to fathom.

How could the object of my pure and boundless love be less than perfect? I could have lived with an embarrassing laugh, a silly taste in music, some limited proclivity for academics. But there was someone else in her life, and she thought that was OK!

I could have fought for her, competed, striven to show her I was the better long-term bet. But the more I got to know her, the more I realized we were poles apart in most values. Now what was I to do with my head-over-heels infatuation? It was difficult, and no amount of preventative medicine will make it easier for you. But I came to realize that I could not have been in love with her, because I didn't know her. And when I got to know her, I didn't choose to love her by my actions.

That wasn't the last time I fell in love. By the time I met your mother, I had learned little about avoiding infatuation. I did know this, however: it would pass. It always does. I'm happy to say that the crush, the rush, the warm fuzzies I felt for your mom were light years ahead of what I had ever felt for anyone before, but if they weren't, that would have been OK too. I wasn't about to marry someone with whom I was hopelessly in love, because that's not a good basis for marriage.

Though I dated your mom for less time than anyone else I had ever dated, and though we were engaged within a few months and married inside a year, ours was the most open and honest and probing relationship I had ever had. This was a woman I knew I would want to love even after I had no choice. You see, when you're in love, you have no say in the matter. Your head and heart tell you that you, among all men, have finally found that perfect vision of looks and personality and character. You think of her all the time, **your** heart races when you talk to her, you want to melt when you touch her.

You don't know her yet.

Now, slow down, don't get excited. I'm not saying in the least that once I got to know my wife, I lost all feelings of love for her. In truth, I feel magnanimously blessed because your mother is so easy to love. But that blind, head-over-heels-puppy-love-crush-infatuation eventually faded as it always does, and love became an action verb instead of a state of being.

Before, when I said, "I love you," I could have just as honestly said, "I'm crazy about you. I idolize you. I can't help myself. You're everything to me."

Now, when I say, "I love you," I could be saying, "I choose to put you ahead of me. I want you to have what you need. I want to do a dirty job you'd rather not do. I want your life to be better because I'm here to make it so. Can I pick up the kids? Can I run an errand? Can I save you some time, some grief, some discomfort? What can I do to act out my love for you?"

OK, I know. You live in this house too, and you know I'm simply not that wonderful. Too often I let Mom act out her love for me and make my life easier. But you see what I'm driving at.

I can't say it too many times. True love, pure love, unconditional love is not something you fall into. Love is an act of the will. Love is as love does. Don't be "in" love. Love.

Now then, unconditional love. Oh boy, could we move on to something else? I thought not.

Unconditional love is divine. Literally. No way we're capable of pure, unconditional love. It's a God concept, and at the risk of seeming flippant, may I say it's one of His best.

God's love is perfect. It is not infatuation. He does not have a crush on us. The Bible doesn't say, "For God was so in love with the world that He gave . . ." Rather the Bible says that God loved us (action verb) in spite of ourselves. He knew all about us and loved us just the same. "God demonstrates His own love toward us, in that while we were still sinners, Christ died for us" (Romans 5:8).

Some translations say God "extended His love toward us," and others say, "God showed His love to us." None say that God was so enamored with us that He was blind to our faults and thought we were wonderful. His is real love, unconditional love, the love of a Creator whose creations have broken His heart. Yet He loves us to the point of death, the death of His Son on the cross.

I wish I could fathom, let alone model or even explain, that kind of love. God loves the unlovable, people no one could like. Another biblical example of that kind of love is the father in Jesus' parable of the prodigal son. That father could not have liked his son. His love for his son is clear, but who could like a boy so selfish that he wants his share now? He wants to leave and do his own thing. He is selfish, wasteful, insensitive.

Today's father, caught in the same bind, would say, "If this money wasn't legally yours, I'd never let you have it. You've been a rotten kid all your life, and now you're going to leave the best situation you could have and squander your fortune."

Do you think it was a surprise to the father of the prodigal that his son returned? I don't. He knew that boy. He watched for him. It wasn't a matter of whether, it was a matter of when. He might have hoped his son would come back happy and prosperous, but he knew better. He couldn't have liked him or liked what he had done, but his love was unconditional.

One of the hardest things the father had to accept was that his son was turning his back on his father's counsel. He would have helped that boy, taught him, shown him, done anything to make him secure. And when the boy returned from dragging his father's name and fortune through pig slop, how did he react? "Oh, sure! You run off against my wishes, squander the fortune I provided for you, and now you come crawling back expecting me to bail you out!"

No, you know the story. There was a ring for his finger, a robe for his back, a fatted calf for his belly. There was even a jealous brother. Unconditional love is worth being jealous of.

What the jealous brother didn't realize, of course, was that he too was loved unconditionally. He simply had shown love for his father by not putting his father's love to such a severe test.

Nothing in life is sadder than unconditional love pushed to its limits. By definition it has no limits, but that is where the supernatural work of God's spirit comes in. Because we are human, finite, frail, we do not have it in us to love unconditionally.

As in romantic love, this love is as this love does. Only God can love someone unconditionally, and we should long to be His instruments in that.

If you've ever seen a twinkle in my eye when we're at odds with each other, you have a hint of the kind of love I want to show to you. I've said more than once, "I love you even when you're ornery." I can correct you, have you be insolent, discipline you for that, let you vent, counsel you on that, let you argue more than I probably should, lecture you about that, all the while comfortable in the knowledge that nothing you can ever say or do will affect the love I have for you.

Hear me, I didn't say that nothing you could ever say or do will affect what I think of you as a person, or what I think of the job we've done raising you, or whether or not I like your person, your character, or your values. I know parents who don't like their kids at all, yet they love them as much as I love you.

You might be surprised to know that I thank God daily that I have kids I like as well as love. It may not always be that way. I won't pretend to like it, or you, if you thumb your nose at your upbringing and set your course on a road of consumption, addiction, materialism, and egotism.

I will not be an enabler. I will not finance a degenerate lifestyle. But nothing you can say or do will affect my love for you. For loving is not a state of being. It's an action verb, an act of the will. Loving is doing.

My prayer and my dream is that you guys will be our best friends all our lives. I look ahead to your college days and your adulthood as times when I'll have to discipline myself to keep my distance. I won't force myself upon you, try to be your buddy, embarrass you in front of your friends.

But you'll know where I am. And we'll talk the way we do now. Nothing is off limits. You can't so disappoint or shock me that the door to conversation is closed. That's all part of love as action.

My friend and mentor Dr. George Sweeting has been a model to me in this. His sons like him and love him and enjoy his company. Three of them have settled near him and all four see him frequently. They revere him too much to lower him to the rank of just a pal, but they are lifelong friends, people who love each other unconditionally.

Loving unconditionally is a risk. Not only do I get close enough to know you well, but you reciprocate. Parents can expect respect and obedience and even a certain amount of familial love. But we are no more worthy of unconditional love than you are. We can't earn it. It isn't a right of parenthood.

Remember this: Love is not a state of being. It's an act of the will. It cannot be demanded or required or commanded. It can only be bestowed.

SET
ONLY
INTRINSIC
GOALS

2

Set Only Intrinsic Goals

Don't feel sorry for me, guys, but it is tough raising sons in a me-first age. It's bad enough that you have to deal with the lusty images Madison Avenue and Hollywood force upon you every day. I thought it was difficult in the sixties when I was a teenager. From the sexual revolution standpoint alone, I would not want to be a teenager today.

But this acquisitive age we live in is every bit as insidious. When I was a boy (I told myself I would never begin a sentence that way when I had kids. Sorry.), self-promotion was frowned upon. Humility was in. Make no mistake, driven people found ways around it. There was maneuvering, posturing, manipulation, behind-the-scenes PR work. People found ways of promoting themselves. If you were too obvious about it you had to be either apologetic or humorous, or you were looked down upon.

That has sure changed. Now people who don't toot their own horns are considered weak, shy, too self-effacing. We're to look out for number one, think of ourselves first (because no one else will), pamper ourselves (because we deserve it). When I was a publishing executive I could have filled a trunk with résumés that contained some variation of the theme "I'm cheerful, hard-working, ambitious, have great ideas, am motivated, a leader, etc., etc."

Even some indirect version of the same would have been better: "My superiors expressed satisfaction with my work and enclosed is a letter of reference."

The tide began turning in the seventies, and by the end of the eighties we had a full-blown traffic jam of self-promoting cads, revving their engines in an attempt to be first through the intersection. Then, to prove they made it, they rewarded themselves with all the trappings. Their T-shirts and bumper stickers read, "The one who dies with the most toys wins." Real funny. Problem is, the one who dies with the most toys is still dead. Don't look for that on a shirt.

The malady, of course, is selfishness and a lack of anything else in which to invest one's life. What a sad target for all they had to offer. Some contributed something to society, and some Christians in this category have even done things beneficial to the kingdom. But what was the motive? Self-promotion. Self-aggrandizement.

The books and tapes and videos aimed at this market have a prevalent thread: There are many, many ways to the top, but the common denominator is goal-orientation. I'm not against setting goals; too many people try to accomplish too much without really knowing their main mission. The problem with the goals I'm talking about is that they are all extrinsic, and all for the benefit of "me."

The avenues to success may all sound good. Take care of your body. Get plenty of sleep. Eat right. Get up early. Read a lot. Write a lot. Know how to talk to people. Learn to sell yourself and your product. Learn to deal with difficult people. Overcome objections. Break down resistance. Work harder. Work smarter. Build a network. Learn to negotiate. Trade favors. Dress right, look right, talk right.

Why? Because you're being paid handsomely and you want to help your company succeed? Because what you're doing benefits others? Because your actions have eternal values and ramifications?

No!

You do all the above because it will bring you what you've always wanted. Notice. Wealth. Success. Self-satisfaction. Leisure time. The ability to travel, to have no financial worries, to be somebody!

Seminars on how to improve your performance in relationships and in the workplace all seem to begin with goal setting. What do you really want in life? Let's see, I want to be making a salary in the six figures by the time I'm twenty-five. I want that dream home before I'm thirty. I want to be company president. I want to own land, companies, a private plane, whatever.

Hear me, boys, I would be proud to see you achieve all that, as long as those were not your goals. Those goals would disappoint me. No, those goals would break my heart. Those goals would tell me where your heart is, and it wouldn't be where God wants it to be.

There is nothing, nothing, nothing wrong with a person's being an achiever or even what society interestingly and probably incorrectly calls an overachiever. God may call you to be famous, a leader, or a wealthy, influential person of independent means. What a responsibility! What an ominous duty! And if you get there because of pure motives and goals, I'll be behind you 100 percent.

I say this before God, however: if you raise a family on lower middle class income because you're a servant of Christ, if you never own a second car, if you can't dress in the latest fashions or take your family out to dinner, let alone entertain anyone else, I will be every bit as proud of you.

Your goals should be intrinsic. Make it your goal to be the best you can be at whatever task is set before you. If my goal from the beginning was to be the best Christian writer in the world, I would be a sad, miserable failure today. I could fill the next several pages with the names of my elders, my contemporaries, and even many up-and-comers who will forever keep me from that selfish goal. I would not enjoy or be inspired and moved by their writing if I saw them only as obstacles to an extrinsic and unrealistic goal.

The goal I have set for myself as a writer is one that must always be striven for and is much more easily measured than the other. I want to be the best writer I can be. If that still places me one hundredth or one thousandth on the list, so be it. It is an achievable goal, and I pray my motive is right. What if I were first on the list and still not the best I could be? That would be tragic, a waste, and not an acceptable offering to God.

Romans 12:1 shows Paul beseeching his readers to present their bodies "a living sacrifice, holy, acceptable to God, which is your reasonable service."

I want to be the best I can be at whatever I am doing, not so that will make me the best in the world and bring me all the goodies outlined above. Rather, I want to present to God a fully exercised measure of that which He has entrusted to me.

Make your goals intrinsic.

If you are called to a place of visibility and your stellar work is recognized, imagine the satisfaction of knowing that you are doing what you're doing for the right motives. If your way of earning a living is secular, it should be for the purpose of advancing the kingdom, both in your workplace and by providing you enough income so that you can support it elsewhere.

One reason I got out of full-time sportswriting was that I was bothered by the dashed hopes of superstars whose goals were misplaced. I wrote sports for a daily paper in the olden days when six-figure pro athletes were just starting to become common. Some wanted to be the first to make two hundred thousand dollars a year, others wanted to be the highest paid on their teams, in their leagues, in history. Others expressed the desire to be "the best there ever was" at a particular position or in a certain sport.

Pity the baseball player who set that as a goal for himself and had to chase the ghost of Babe Ruth around the bases every night. Pity the basketball player who wants to be the best ever and knows he'll never crack anyone's all-time top five.

I saw athletes with what appeared to be limitless gifts and potential who were satisfied to be the best in their leagues. A player for the Chicago White Sox in the late sixties and early seventies could very well have been the first .400 hitter since Ted Williams. He was so satisfied with a big contract and a .310 average that he didn't even take batting practice every day.

Think of it! A man who, without working hard, could hit .310 and run like a gazelle who didn't care to be the best he could be because he was already as good as he needed to be. St. Louis Cardinal fans will recall an outfielder so talented he could not be removed from the line-up, yet so lazy he couldn't make it all the way in to the dugout between innings unless he was sure to hit. He sat in the bullpen otherwise!

I covered high school baseball players who loved the game and had certain gifts but who had no business even dreaming of professional careers. Yet when they were finally released after having reached double A or triple A or even playing a few big league games, they were rightfully and justifiably satisfied. Why? Because their goal had been to be the best they could be. If that meant making it, they would make it. If that meant going two or three levels higher than anyone thought they would by sheer desire, hustle, and discipline, that was all right too.

Some would look at a player like that and say, "Too bad. He failed. How embarrassing."

Yet those players move on to the next challenge in life and strive to be the best they can be at it, whether it makes them company president or rank-and-file worker, and they know they've succeeded.

Don't set quantitative goals, boys. Set qualitative goals. Don't say I'm going to do this or be that or make this or achieve that by a certain age or date. I know that goes against all conventional wisdom and that motivational speakers say, "I never met a successful person who didn't set goals." All I'm saying is: set the right goals and with the right motives.

People ask me, "How many books do you want to write?" Would you believe I've never thought about it? The only reason I count the ones I've done is because people seem to want to know. I know it's an unusual amount, and I can't pretend not to enjoy the attention it can bring. But I would rather be known as a pro than as prolific. I'd rather people know I do the best I can do on each than that they know how many I have "cranked out." How I hate that term! If I could crank them out, I would.

An adjunct to the goal of doing the best you can do at whatever it is you are doing is to specialize. There is a temptation to be a Renaissance man, to show that besides this you can also do that. Better to be the best you can be at one thing than to be above average (or worse) at several.

As you know, part of my work includes speaking. I enjoy it, and sometimes the audience enjoys it. I don't want to be falsely modest, but it is not my calling. I'm not trained for or comfortable in the pulpit, so I do banquets and conferences. I strive to do the best I can do at each opportunity, but it does not frustrate me to know that I will never be in demand like the great speakers of my day. Sometimes when I do the best I'm capable of doing, something special happens. God works, and I enjoy having been used.

But I know my limitations. Though as a writer I am not the "best there ever was" either, that's my calling, and that's where I concentrate. I don't sing or dance or preach. I guess that's why I write so much. It's all I do.

If you make a million dollars a year, I hope it is because your goal was to be the best you could be at whatever made you the million, and not because you write that figure at the top of your calendar every day for a year.

If you become famous and sought after, I hope it's because your goal was to glorify God and serve Him and others.

If you do indeed become the best there ever was at your profession, I hope it's because you made the decision early to give yourself, all of yourself, to Christ.

We know who we are and who we are not. Spiritually we are depraved and worthless, and yet God showed His love to us in that while we were still sinners, Christ died for us. And what can we offer in return?

Normally I'm not one to stack proof-text verses, but humor me here and catch the drift of what Scripture has to say about the value of our repayment:

"But we are all like an unclean thing, and all our righteousnesses are like filthy rags; we all fade as a leaf, and our iniquities, like the wind, have taken us away" (Isaiah 64:6).

"For I say to you, that unless your righteousness exceeds the righteousness of the scribes and Pharisees, you will by no means enter the kingdom of heaven" (Matthew 5:20).

"Not by works of righteousness which we have done, but according to His mercy He saved us, through the washing of regeneration and renewing of the Holy Spirit" (Titus 3:5).

"For by grace you have been saved through faith, and that not of yourselves; it is the gift of God, not of works, lest anyone should boast" (Ephesians 2:8-9).

So what do we have to offer?

Nothing.

Then why present our bodies as living sacrifices?

In gratitude.

When I bought you a bike and you brought me a handful of dandelions, you weren't repaying me. You were thanking me. And those otherwise worthless weeds were precious to me. Figuratively, if not literally, they were a sweet fragrance to me because they came from a pure, innocent, grateful heart that had no capacity to really repay.

And I didn't want or expect any repayment. I wanted to show my love, and I cherished your childlike expression of thanks.

That's what we have to offer God: lives framed by goals that are not self-driven but are qualitative, intrinsic, and right-motivated.

WE
NEVER
QUIT

3

WE NEVER QUIT

I wish I could make this one sound more spiritual. There is a biblical basis for it. As soon as you see the verse, you'll roll your eyes and say, "Now here's one we knew was coming because we've heard it every other day for as long as we can remember."

Ready?

"Go to the ant, you sluggard! Consider her ways and be wise, which, having no captain, overseer or ruler, provides her supplies in the summer, and gathers her food in the harvest. How long will you slumber, O sluggard? When will you rise from your sleep?" (Proverbs 6:6-9).

Were you right, or did you think this was my evidence for not letting you sleep in? No, this is not my usual diatribe about laziness. I see the ant not just as the antithesis of a sluggard but also as one who never quits.

When I was a boy (there I go again), I say to my shame that I sometimes participated in unspeakable evil to creatures. I did not have the guts to put a cherry bomb in a frog's mouth or light the fuse, but I watched and didn't interfere. I kicked a toad around the yard once for no reason.

My best friend and I even held a magnifying glass between an ant and the sun and saw it try to scramble to safety before shriveling to a crisp. I know. It was awful, and it does not absolve me to admit it here. Neither does it make me feel any better to know that most little boys do such things just for the experience, or maybe because we are, by nature, evil.

But I digress.

Once I grew tired of terrorizing ants and merely watched them for an hour. You've done this. You know it's fascinating. They are relentless and hard working. They carry several times their body weights, they work together, they stick with a job, and they get it done. I saw maybe five or six dozen ants working, working, working, building an ant hill.

Now what I did next was just short of being as cruel as killing them, and my only defense is that I did this out of pure and almost innocent curiosity. The fact is, I still feel guilty, but I did learn a lesson. I didn't get punished, as I should have, but that was only because I didn't confess it to the proper person (sorry, Dad, but I think the statute of limitations has passed by now).

As I watched from my prone position a couple of feet above the ant hill (our front yard had a low, concrete wall I hung over to watch such activities in the grass next to the sidewalk), I waited until the inch-and-a-half-high hill was almost finished. Amazingly, they had made it smooth and symmetrical. It was a thing of beauty, and I had no business defiling it. At least I didn't kill or, as far as I know, even injure any more ants.

I reached down and formed my middle finger and thumb in the classic marble shooting position and made one major flick at the base of the hill. Those few ants still in the chute on their way underground went rolling and tumbling in the grass with what was left of their labors. If ants could swear, those babies were cussing me out good. It wouldn't surprise me if they were shaking their little ant fists at me. *Creepo fat little kid,* they'd mutter.

More ants than I knew were even in there came pouring out of the ground, and I had visions of them marshaling some bees and wasps and other hideous and offense-minded carnivores and chasing me into the house. But in reality they never looked at me.

Without missing a beat, they began to work again. They seemed to organize, form lines, assign tasks, and begin building again. My first thought was that they were stupid, as stupid as mosquitoes, who can't see the smear of their compatriot on my arm and know they're about to realize the same fate. Why can't insects see the odds, recognize corpses, and move on?

If the ants had, they would not have so ably served this illustration. They didn't quit. They never gave up. They didn't even slow down. Not one of them, as far as I know, said, "All right, that's it. We slave all afternoon, and this sleazoid destroys our house for no reason. Forget it. What's the use? I quit."

No. No quitting.

My dad never let me quit either. If injuries can be psychosomatic, mine were, and if people can be temporarily accident prone, I was when I broke my arm as a freshman football player. I was a big kid, but baseball was my game. I loved watching football, but the work was too hard, the attitude too coarse, the ones who loved to hit too crazy. Two-a-day practices in the August sun were more than I could take.

I was an athlete. In shape, strong, fast. I should have done well as a football player. But I dreaded it. Maybe I would have liked it when the actual games began, but meanwhile, it was suicide drills, kamikaze exercises. Who was toughest, who was craziest, who would do the most smashing and banging and life-risking stunts to prove he was the meanest?

Problem was, even though I took naps at home after the grueling morning workout and had bad dreams about the one coming up, counting the minutes, of one thing I was certain: Dad would not let me quit. We're Jenkinses. We don't quit. We start something, we see it through. We take on responsibility, we fulfill it.

Ironically, I would have started and probably done well on that team, as much as I hated it. I would not allow my distaste for the game to come through as cowardice or hesitation, at least so that it showed. Perhaps a touch of those hazardous traits found their way to the surface when I tackled one of the heaviest players on the team. My forearm was embedded behind his knee when he squatted and vice-snapped it before hitting the ground.

I was relieved! It hurt. It was a nuisance. But it was the only way I could have quit.

This is not a treatise on subconsciously self-inflicted injuries. I didn't purposely place my arm behind Hubbard Helms's gigantic leg. I was tackling the way they told me to, and I was one of the few who could wrestle the big man to the ground. (To further illustrate the concentration camp ambiance of these workouts, it should be noted that this was more than fifteen years before William Perry became the first massive lineman to carry the ball. Helms would never carry the ball in a game. He was a lineman. But in practice we readied ourselves for hitting little backs by trying to tackle big non-backs.)

What a disappointment. I had to quit football. I never went back. I played a lot of baseball and pickup basketball and intramurals of all sorts, but I didn't have the dedication to football that would have made me successful. (That's a nice way of saying that despite my size I wasn't much of a macho banger.)

You know what, though? Even those few weeks of torture were helpful to me. I'm glad I didn't just give up. I'm glad my dad made me stick with it for all the right reasons. He knew I wasn't a sissy or a weakling, but he didn't make me stick with it to prove that. He made me stick with it because we simply didn't quit. Family policy.

Table games. You start Monopoly and within half an hour you're begging for mercy, trying to sell Get Out of Jail Free cards for face value, trading a free trip around the board for future concessions. You want to quit? Forget it. You started, you finish. Take it like a man. You may be wiped out, passing your last single dollars across the board to your big brother (choke), but you leave the game when it is over and not before. Why?

Because you implied that you would when you sat down to play. It was an unwritten contract. You give the victor the satisfaction of a worthy, enduring opponent. We were not even allowed to slack off at the end of a table tennis game if we were down 20-2.

It was considered bad sportsmanship to quit or even to switch to lackadaisical play.

And you know what sometimes happens? The worm turns. The table turns. I've seen nearly bankrupt Monopolists get lucky. All they have left are the railroads and a couple of mortgaged monopolies, and suddenly no one else can land anywhere but on those hated tracks. The poor man gets Community Chests and Go to Jails and Chances that keep him dancing between hoteled properties, and suddenly he has enough to unmortgage, to start charging rent. Then he lands on Free Parking, and even though Parker Brothers advises against stockpiling riches in the center of the board for the lucky lander in the parking lot, you do it anyway. And who gets it? He who needs it most. Hotels are rebuilt, the rich get poorer, and the poor get richer.

Now, admittedly, for every time that happens there are countless times when not quitting means just gritting your teeth and sticking it out. I wanted to quit a paper route on which I helped my best friend. It was a huge route, more than a hundred sixty papers, daily plus Saturday and that monster Sunday rag.

When I signed on I had no idea what it would be like to face that responsibility every night after school, every Saturday afternoon, and horror of horrors, every Sunday morning before the sun came up. That paper was so big you had to come back to the drop-off point to refill your bag. There was no taking half the route's Sunday papers in one trip and Dan's taking the other.

I was young enough to be afraid of the dark, forevermore, and there I was trudging around the community in the eerie pre-dawn, weighed down with papers.

Why couldn't I quit? I didn't need the money. I had thought it would be fun. I saw Dan only at the start and the finish. Dad, please, why not?

You made a commitment. It's a duty. You said you would. You will. You don't quit.

But I saved all the money I wanted to save. I bought the ball glove. How long do I have to do this?

No quitting.

How long did it take before I was used to it? I grew stronger, faster at it, developed some routines. Dan and I competed to see who could finish his half first each day. The winner got to choose which half of the route to take the next day. I learned there was nothing in the darkness that was not there during the light.

I still remember stomping through snowdrifts, ice forming on the scarf over my mouth, aching muscles, freezing fingers (you can't fold a paper with gloves on), and telling myself with each step, "You can't quit."

I wanted to quit. I would get mad and wonder if Dad knew how grueling this was. I was a kid, not even a teenager yet. One lesson I learned: all the time I really and truly and sincerely wanted to quit, I never stopped taking the next step. Had I stopped and sat down or collapsed or leaned against a tree to cry or just feel sorry for myself, I might be there still. I kept moving. I knew if I quit I would have to make the long trek home anyway.

And I certainly couldn't quit in the middle of the route. Then Dan would have to do it. And he would have to do it himself until he found a replacement. And we probably wouldn't remain best friends. How could we after I let him down that way?

So I kept moving, resenting the papers, resenting the route, resenting Dan, resenting Dad. But not quitting. I tried not to think about where I was on the route and how far I still had to go. By not quitting and not even stopping, the yet-to-delivers gradually became the already-delivereds, and finally it was over.

Where did the energy come from to race toward the ending point with Dan in sight at the other end of the block? We argued about who finished first, threw snowballs at each other, swung empty bags at each other, and ran most of the way home. It was so good to be done. Dan was such a good friend. I never wanted to forget those days. And I haven't.

I was in my hometown just the other day, and I drove that paper route. Back came the old fears of missing someone, not having enough papers, remembering which house to deliver to. I thought the route would look small and innocent like so many other landmarks did, but it was just as ominous and forbidding as always.

But what a sweet memory. I'm so glad I didn't quit.

That maxim carries me now even in minor matters such as losing something. That can be maddening, but I find myself stubbornly refusing to give up. I will not quit looking. While trying to fix something myself—which a repairman could do in a minute—I may find a wire that takes a surgeon's hand to reattach. The more I fail to make the connection, the more stubborn I become. Someone might even suggest a simpler way. Not now. I started it, I'll finish it.

That kind of single-minded obsession may be more a middle-aged man's idiosyncrasy than anything else, but I'll tell you this: it has carried me through many a book that had more pages left to write than had been written. Rather than look at the whole, at the few pages stacked on the table and the many that needed to be produced, I just kept plodding. I couldn't quit. Family policy.

When I was seven, they tell me, I swam like a fish. I once swam a couple of hundred feet to a raft where my mother was chatting with other parents. I accepted the accolades for having come so far and being so brave, but in the next twenty minutes the raft drifted more than half way across the lake.

When I moved to dive in and swim back to shallow waters, now a long, long way off, some asked me if I was sure I could make it. I probably should not have tried. I wanted to prove that the trip out was no fluke, so I dived and began swimming, pacing myself for the long haul. I was in the deepest part of the lake, and I did not want to go back to the raft, though the shore seemed to get farther away as I swam.

I remember feeling good about not panicking, though I was tired. I knew there was no choice. When I was finally closer to the shore than to the raft, there was no going back. Panicking would kill me because no one could reach me in time, even if they heard me.

I settled in to that slow, steady pace and just kept swimming. My mother kept an eye on me, of course, but no one else noticed. Back near the beach the other kids romped and frolicked, unaware I had even been gone. I was tired but not exhausted, and as I reached the pier, gathering my strength, I knew I had accomplished something. The key was in not quitting.

That same policy served the summer I graduated from high school. I got a job working construction. I was an unskilled laborer in the hot sun, the only way available to pay my way to college. I dreaded the morning, was too bone weary to relax when I got home, didn't have the energy to play ball or even go out with my friends. Could I last ten weeks?

I wanted to quit, but beside the fact that my dad wouldn't let me anyway, I knew I had no options. If I didn't do that job and make that money and go to college, I would have to work like that the rest of my life. There's nothing wrong with that except it wasn't what I wanted to do.

Within ten days I was healthier, stronger, full of energy. The job no longer dominated my waking and sleeping hours. I was back in circulation, playing ball, running with my friends, enjoying life, and saving for college. Those ten weeks paid for my first year; sad to say you'd have to be a corporation president to do the same today. Just like the paper route, while it never became my favorite thing to do, it was a valuable shaper of attitudes.

But that's why you hear me say it all the time, for important things and not seemingly so important things: We don't quit.

They say Winston Churchill once spoke to the graduating class of a boys' school and simply said, "Never give in. Never give in. Never, never, never give in," and sat down to a thunderous ovation.

Whether the story is true, and if so whether the boys were simply thrilled to have had to endure only a short speech, I can't say. But it's an inspiring tale nonetheless. No compromise, no gilding, no explanation. Just never give up. Don't quit.

Don't forget it.

**SOME
PEOPLE
HAVE THE
RIGHT
TO BE
WRONG**

4

SOME PEOPLE HAVE
THE RIGHT TO BE WRONG

Before I get into another reason to never quit, I am compelled to remind you that I know I'm no paragon relating to this list. I believe these truths and I urgently want you to listen, hear, understand, and apply them, but I confess I learned too many of these the hard way.

The parent in me wants you to learn from my mistakes, allow me to be the one with the knocks and bruises. Then all you have to do is get in line and sail through life. The adult in me knows better. Many of the mistakes I made were violations of axioms and maxims my parents tried to impress upon my brothers and me. Maybe we should have simply believed and understood and followed, but I'm certain the lessons would not be as deeply ingrained.

So why do I bother if you're going to charge out ahead and learn the hard way anyway? Just so I can say I told you so? No. It's because early in the stages of frustration and remorse you'll recall that someone before you made the same mistake, learned from it, grew from it. Failure is no reason to quit the game, even if you should have known better.

One of my favorite songs is one that was never as widely known as most written by Bill and Gloria Gaither. I've had the fun of interviewing them both and asking them to quote it for me. Neither can get through it. Oh, they remember the lyrics. It's just that they're also parents of three, and these are more than just words to them.

I present them here with their permission:

I Wish You

I wish you some springtime, some "bird on the wing time"
For blooming and sending out shoots;
I wish you some test time, some winter and rest time
For growing and putting down roots.

I wish you some summer, for you're a becomer,
With blue skies and flowers and dew;
For there is a reason God sends every season:
He's planted His image in you.

I wish you some laughter, some "happy thereafter"
To give you a frame for your dreams;
But I wish you some sorrows, some rainy tomorrows,
Some clouds with some sun in between.

I wish you some crosses, I wish you some losses,
For only in losing you win;

I wish you some growing, I wish you some knowing
There's always a place to begin.

We'd like to collect you and shield and protect you,
And save you from hurts if we could;
But we must let you grow tall, to learn and know all
That God has in mind for your good.

We never could own you, for God only loaned you
To widen our world and our hearts.
So, we wish you His freedom, knowing where He is leading,
There is nothing can tear us apart.*

Truth number five, which I want you to always remember: Some people have the right to be wrong.

This one's no fun. People in authority, with responsibility, have the right to be wrong. Society can function in
no other way. Now, by wrong, I don't mean they have the
right to break the law or inflict bodily injury or make you
do the same. But they have the right to be shortsighted,
foolish, disagreeable, unfair, rigid, and stubborn.

Some people have the right to do things the way they
think they should be done, rather than the way you or I
think they should be done. Each of us has built-in confidence that our way is best. Maybe that's true the first day
or two on a new job, but once we've had a little experience, watched the admired veterans do it, and selected the
best procedures, we know what would work best. It may
even happen that we are right. We may be a little more
widely read or traveled than the boss, have a little more
common sense or intelligence, and we're right.

I once drove a fork-lift truck in a factory. The first few
days I was all thumbs and rode the brake a lot to keep

---

* © Copyright 1975 by William J. Gaither. International Copyright se-
cured. All rights reserved. Used by permission.

from knocking over things and people. But soon the controls became second nature to me, and I could maneuver that baby as if it were part of me. It was fun. I disciplined myself to drive slowly enough that I could react if someone stepped in front of me.

This was a loud place where nails were made from huge bales of wire. My job was to lift these bales from a central location and thread my way through the various machine stations to replace empty spools. Now I'm referring to five- and six-foot spools two feet in diameter. The empty spools might weight fifty pounds, but the full ones weighed hundreds.

I had great fun speeding into the central location, knifing one of the forks into the top of a spooled bale of wire, spinning the truck around, and making my delivery. My goal was to set down the new spool, move the old one into the aisle, set the new on in place, and take the empty back, all with the fork-lift.

When I was new at it, it might have taken less time to handle the empty spool by hand, but I was taught to do it with the machine. That would be easier and quicker in the end.

What was wrong was how the supervisor told me to drive the fork-lift. He said that when I had made the switch, I should back the truck all the way to the spool supply, then turn around and select one and head back out.

I was young and naive, but I was not stupid. I knew there had to be a reason for such an absurdity. Maybe it was safety. Maybe he thought a young fork-lift operator didn't know how to turn around in a narrow aisle where people worked close by. So I asked him.

"Are you afraid I'll hit someone? Because actually I'd be more likely to hit someone trying to drive the thing backwards that far."

"Just do it like I told ya."

"You know the truck is faster and easier to steer going forward."

"Just do it like I told ya."

"Could I ask why? I mean, I'd hate to hit anyone or get less done because—"

"Just do it like I told ya."

"Well, I will if you insist, but I've been turning around in the aisle, and it's been working fine, so—"

"Are you gonna do it like I told ya, or am I gonna hafta get somebody else to do it?"

I did it like he told me. This would make a great illustration if I could tell you of some horrible accident that happened because I or someone else decided he knew better than the boss. But the fact is, he was simply wrong. I had several near misses on that job because I was required to back the fork-lift truck several hundred feet through the factory.

I discussed it with other drivers. They all rolled their eyes and shrugged and shook their heads.

"That's the way Peppy did it in his day, and he can't see there's a better way."

Peppy's way was wrong, inefficient, dangerous, and —I'm so happy to be able to put this on paper after all these years—stupid. But Peppy had a right to be wrong. He was the boss. I had to do it his way or lose my job.

You guys have faced that with teachers and coaches. Of course, most of the time teachers and coaches are right, and when I was a boy (wink), we were not allowed to question them. I still hate questioning them. You'll recall that the only time I interfered with a coach is when he tried to tell one of you to throw off the wrong foot. Even then I was courteous and pleaded with him to try to recall if he'd ever seen any right-hander throw while stepping with his right foot.

It's obnoxious, and you're being insolent, when you argue with a person in authority on a matter of opinion. If the coach thinks you were goofing around and tells you to run five laps, run the five laps even if you know he was wrong.

"But it wasn't me" is only going to get you five more.

If he puts the wrong defender on the other team's big man, you may feel you have every right to suggest another course. When you're a coach, you be magnanimous and tell the team, "Now if anyone has a better idea, let's hear it." Unless your coach asks, do it his way. It's his responsibility. Even when he is wrong and you are right and everybody knows it, some people have the right to be wrong.

When a teacher disciplines the whole class for the actions of one, and it's unfair, remember that that classroom is the teacher's domain. Again, if a person in authority acts illegally or unethically, you have no responsibility to condone that or do likewise. But if it's just a matter of opinion, obey and shut up.

Why? For one thing, there's no future in arguing. People in charge resent it. Sometimes, even when they ask for input, they don't really want it. You have to learn to know when your differing opinion is truly being sought.

Primarily, living with other people's mistakes is part of life. You will have teachers, bosses, relatives, officials, all kinds of people in charge who make mistakes or who are simply wrong. Am I telling you to become yes-men? No. Not until a directive has been given. Then, yes, support it.

I tried to impress upon my work teams, when I was in a decision-making position, that I wanted their input, agreeable or not, until I had issued a directive. Then I wanted their support.

There were times when I went against the best counsel of the majority of my managers—usually to my regret—but I had to learn that lesson myself. It would have been counterproductive for someone to say, "Well, you'll recall I was against it from the beginning. I pushed you to the wall, and the majority was with me, but you followed your hunch, and it failed. Don't count me as part of this flop."

I've been on the other end of that too. I've sat on boards or under supervisors where my opinion was in the minority, though it was proved right later. The temptation is to remind people of that because, believe me, they will not remember. There will be no, "Boy, we sure wish we'd listened to Jenkins."

Resist the urge to rub it in. The person in authority had the responsibility, is accountable, is compensated, and will have to answer for his decisions. He has the right to be wrong. Offer polite counsel, then keep your mouth shut and do your job. If we quit in a huff every time the boss did something wrong, none of us would have jobs.

You will come to know many people who flit from job to job and career to career. They will be the ones who talk about their dumb bosses, the stupid policies, the unfair practices. Somehow, these people never find anyone to work for who is as brilliant as they are.

This also falls under the category of the truth in the next chapter (Life Isn't Fair), so I urge you to long remember: Some people have the right to be wrong.

LIFE
ISN'T
FAIR

5

LIFE ISN'T FAIR

Among the saddest lessons I've ever had to learn is that life isn't fair. The rich get richer. The poor get poorer. Nice people suffer. Bad people prosper. It's truth as old as Scripture itself:

"Righteous are You, O Lord, when I plead with You; yet let me talk with You about Your judgments. Why does the way of the wicked prosper? Why are those happy who deal so treacherously?" (Jeremiah 12:1).

I'm not sure why, but I have less of a problem with wicked people prospering than I do with righteous people suffering. I know that, in fact, there are no truly righteous people. But you know of genuinely humble, devout, consistent believers who suffer more than most. It's enough to make anyone of even modest means feel guilty.

You have two dear relatives, men now long past middle-age, to whom life has been most unfair. One was raised without a father. The other lost his older brother in a fiery auto crash when he was a teenager. One reached the top of his profession, even to the point of becoming head of the trade organization for all his peers. The governor of the state attended his installation.

Yet false rumors besmirched his reputation. He moved on to greener pastures that dried up and blew away. He was stricken physically, and his job was eliminated while he fought to recover. He eventually took a job he was overqualified for and became, in essence, a rank-and-file member of the profession he once headed.

He is a humble, generous, gentle man. He does not complain. Those of us who love him complain for him. It isn't fair. Life has not treated him right. It never will. Life is not fair.

The other relative worked carefully and diligently for a business all his adult life. He rose to the top echelons and fully expected to be named president of the company when his superior retired. He had not been inappropriately ambitious. He had been meticulous and industrious. He was widely respected.

A consulting firm was engaged to study the company and its multifaceted operations. For several months everyone was interviewed at length, from the brass to entry-level workers. The conclusion was that this man was eminently qualified, smart, experienced, and, best of all, admired and respected by colleagues and subordinates. The recommendation of the consultants: make this man your president immediately.

The decision of the board of directors: The son of the previous president should rise three levels to take the helm. To those who didn't know that the son was a lazy, incompetent goldbrick, it was revealed within eighteen months—the time it took for the wrong choice of a leader to bring the company to the brink of bankruptcy.

Ironically, the man who should have been chosen left the company in disappointment, knowing he was past the age when anyone else would select him as president. He joined a consulting firm that was eventually called in to rescue the original firm, and he was key to the adjustment process.

Still, life had not been fair to him. That bit of recompense served little more than to prove that the wrong decision had been made. It didn't really make up for it.

You know our dear friends the Tippits. Sammy is an international evangelist. His wife, Tex, is a model partner, a prayer warrior, a true compatriot in the ministry. Their children, David and Renee, have been all over the world with them, ministering in the hard places where no one else seems to want to go.

They are not perfect people, but they are sold out. They live on faith. Sammy has passed up comfortable salaries in any one of the several huge churches that would call him as their pastor. But the Tippits' values are not material. They live in a modest home, wear modest clothes, drive a used car. Their values are eternal.

Sammy has had cancer.

Tex has come through serious surgery.

David nearly choked to death as an infant and suffered convulsions later.

Renee was hit by a car in eastern Europe.

You may ask, Why them and not us? We can't say our priorities are as firm as theirs. Surely our callings and choices have been cushier. Why then would God allow them to suffer so?

Selfless people give up everything to go to the mission field, only to lose a spouse or a child or to suffer some form of debilitating disease. Why? We don't know why. Life isn't fair.

By saying life isn't fair, are we saying God isn't fair? God chooses not to defend Himself, not even to Job. Job claims in Job 12:6 that the "tents of robbers prosper, and those who provoke God are secure." God merely asks Job (Job 38:4), "Where were you when I laid the foundations of the earth? Tell Me, if you have understanding."

In the previous chapter I spoke to the fact that some people have the right to be wrong. Well, we know God by His very nature and definition is right even when He appears to be wrong.

I will not question His sovereignty, and I dare not expect Him to run His universe the way I might run it (imagine that!). We puny, finite beings might wash John 14:6 from the Book and let anyone into the kingdom who seemed like a nice, sincere person. We might have told the men in the parable of the worker that those who worked the longest would make the most and those who came late would be paid accordingly.

That would have been fair, but it certainly wouldn't have been an accurate picture of redemption, for that's what that parable was all about. See the payment as the reward of heaven, and see the day's work as coming to Christ. Are you qualified for a larger measure of grace because you came to Christ as a child, as opposed to a murderer who came to Him on his deathbed?

God is fairer than fair, exceedingly, abundantly generous.

The Tippits, the missionaries, our relatives, all those who have accepted what seem to us unfair blows in this life, will get their rewards in the next.

When you find yourself wondering why it is that children suffer abuse and that scoundrels, due to technicalities, get off of serious charges when they are clearly guilty, remember this point. It isn't something you can rest in or understand. It is merely something to accept. Life isn't fair. No one said it would be.

You know when this is driven home to me (pardon the pun in advance)? On the highway. Some years ago, when I got a new car, I decided that I would buckle up every time I got in and I would drive the speed limit. Right on the button. Use the cruise control and set it precisely where the signs said.

For four years I was a stickler on that. I confess I caused a few traffic jams by insisting on going the speed limit. People aren't too accepting, even if you're in the far right lane. And now I pretty much go with the flow, rarely letting myself get much past five over the limit.

But those four years changed the way I drive. I used to compete, get angry, even vindictive. I took other driver's offenses personally. Now, because of that exercise and how long I kept it up, I am able to let other drivers be as crazy and brazen and rude as they want to be. I stay out of their way and do nothing to further infuriate them, or myself.

In fact, I'm courteous. When lanes merge, I alternate and let someone in. I still get irritated when signs for more than a mile have warned that a lane is closed and yet people stay right there, expecting everyone to let them in when the rest of us have dutifully got in line. Sometimes in that case I will maintain some righteous indignation, and let them work for it.

But even when I am being wonderful and generous, how often is kindness reciprocated? If I alternate and let a car, or two, or three off a ramp ahead of me onto a busy expressway, say even every day for a solid week, what happens when I am the one on the ramp?

Does anyone, anyone, alternate and let me in? Hardly ever.

Life isn't fair.

That may seem a trivial example, but it's indicative. It's a reminder that we should do the right thing because it's the right thing and not because we will ever be repaid.

That could almost be a thirteenth thing I want you to remember forever. Do we do the right thing because everybody else does? Do we do the right thing because we'll be embarrassed if we get caught not doing it? Do we do the right thing only in public? No, we do the right thing because it's the right thing. Life is not fair, but we will not change that by being unfair ourselves. (We won't change it by being fair either, but we will impact the people in our own little orbits.)

I was fortunate to be raised by parents who truly believed that two wrongs do not make a right. There was no cottoning to vengeance. None of: "Well, since he did this, I'll do that. He deserves it. It serves him right."

Take a hot dish to the church potluck. Someone carelessly breaks the bowl, knowing full well it's yours. You are neither informed nor recompensed. So next time you'll know better, won't you?

To show them, you won't bring a dish next time. You'll just eat your fill and make up for the loss that way. No, you'll bring food, but it won't be anything special. It'll be something your family hates. And you won't take it in a nice dish. You'll send it in a plastic container. See if they can ruin that! And see if you care if they do!

That scenario would have been foreign in our house. My mother would have come back to the next potluck with a larger, better dish and even better food. Trying to heap coals of fire on the head of the guilty? No. Just doing the right thing because it's the right thing.

You've given money to a cause, and now the board of directors of that organization has elected a leader you can't stand. You can withdraw your support, making life difficult for the workers who count on your giving and injuring the overall ministry. Or you can do the right thing because it's the right thing and not lower yourself to whatever level at which you consider the new leader resides.

You lend a vehicle to your youth group, and it's returned low on gas, with a tear in the upholstery and full of empty pop cans and snack bags. Do you refuse to lend it again? Is that the right thing?

Let me be clear: I'm not suggesting that you don't speak forthrightly to the person in charge. There's a major difference between doing the right thing because life isn't fair and letting yourself get walked on because you aren't bold enough to be honest. Someone should be taken to task for the poor treatment of your property, but to withhold your generosity to even the score would be to contribute to the axiom of this chapter.

When I wrote George Sweeting's biography, I titled it *A Generous Impulse,* not only because of his appreciation for the phrase "Seldom repress a generous impulse," but also because his life was a shining example of that.

In his years as an evangelist, pastor, and president of the Moody Bible Institute, Dr. Sweeting had many experiences of unfair treatment. Detractors talked behind his back, people he reprimanded criticized him. People he had to let go said hurtful things about him publicly. Yet he never retaliated, never defended himself.

In fact, when recommending severance packages and considerations for people who considered themselves his enemies (though he would never refer to them as such), he was consistently generous almost to a fault.

He did the right thing because it was the right thing and did not repay evil for evil. He knew life was not fair and didn't expect it to be. I want you to remember that forever, not so you live in depression and cynicism but so you will not be so disappointed and will live in a way that will make a difference.

TAKE
RESPONSIBILITY
FOR
YOUR
OWN
ACTIONS

6

TAKE RESPONSIBILITY FOR YOUR OWN ACTIONS

I handed a piece of luggage to a baggage handler at O'Hare, but when he took it, I didn't let go quickly enough. The bag shifted, got away from both of us, and hit the floor on one of its corners. It fell open, and my photo and sound equipment rattled out across the corridor.

It wasn't his fault, but rather than apologizing to simply express his regret over my embarrassment and inconvenience, or even scrambling to help pick everything up and make sure it was not damaged (it wasn't), the man defended himself.

As I crawled around gathering up tapes and film and equipment, he spewed out his explanation.

"I didn't do that! You held on too long!"

"No problem," I said. "My fault."

I confess I said that in the hope that he would join me and finish the task quickly. He did not.

"Yup, you held on too long," he repeated. "That wasn't me."

I was angrier at his refusal to accept any responsibility than at the ordeal of having to retrieve all my stuff. At least it wasn't underwear.

I didn't say it was his fault, and I didn't want him to say it was his fault. We two had mishandled something. Surely each of us has had enough experience handing heavy items to another. The receiver has a responsibility to not turn away with it until he is sure he alone has it. The deliverer has a responsibility to release the item once he has passed it on. Was it important who contributed most to the mishap?

I was nearly finished when a woman behind the counter noticed and hurried to my aid. "I'm so sorry this happened," she said, as if she had done it herself. We both knew she had nothing to do with it, so clearly she was simply expressing sympathy. She was sorry for me, not for herself.

She gave her co-worker a look, as if expecting him to say or do something. All he did was repeat, "I didn't do that. He held on too long."

Her smile froze. "No one says you did it, and no one cares. We're just sorry it happened, aren't we? And aren't we eager to help straighten it out?"

By then she and I were done. If that man won't share responsibility, imagine how he reacts when he is at fault.

Passing the blame has to be one of our earliest and basest defense mechanisms. Where do we learn to distance ourselves from blame so early? It wasn't me—it was him! I didn't do it—she did! Don't blame me! It's not my fault! Even Adam said, "It was the woman you gave me!"

"Well, I woulda brought my book home, but the coach didn't give us enough time to go back to our lockers and—"

"She made me forget."

"He wouldn't lend me a pencil."

"No one knew what time it was."

"I didn't know you were here."

But that kind of talk doesn't end when childhood ends. "Why didn't the magazine get published on time?"

"We didn't get the pages to the printer on time."

"Why?"

"Because the editors didn't get their corrections to the production manager in time."

"Why?"

"Because one was sick and the others had to cover for him and they got behind."

"Why didn't they find help or work overtime?"

"They didn't know anyone was available."

"Why didn't they ask their superiors?"

"Because they didn't think the superiors would do that kind of work."

"Why didn't the superiors make it clear in advance that they would help out in such emergencies?"

Will someone stop here and take personal responsibility for something? People pass and pass and pass the buck and then see it passed right back. Supervisors can go months without once hearing someone say, "That was my fault. I messed up. I forgot. I'll make it right."

I still remember one of my first experiences with a full-time job. My boss asked me if a certain story had been sent to the typesetter yet. Immediately I felt my voice constrict and grow higher. I had to speak louder to make the sound come out.

"I was on a long distance call," I said. "And I had to get those pictures to the darkroom."

He smiled.

"Has the story been sent to the typesetter?"

"Well, I was gonna do that as soon as I got back from the darkroom."

"Are you back?"

"Yes, sir."

"Have you sent the story?"

"No, sir."

"Are you going to do it right now?"

"Yes, sir."

I began to get to it.

"One more question," he said.

"Sir?"

"Do you see how this conversation could have been edited?"

"Sir?"

"Shortened to my first question and your last answer?"

I nodded. He had asked if the story had been sent. I should have said, "I'm sending it right now."

If he wanted any more detail, like why it had not already been done, then I could have told him.

What would I have said today, more than twenty years after the fact? I would not have explained. I would have simply taken the blame. "I'm sending it right now."

"Why has it not already been sent?"

"That was my fault. I got behind, but I'll take care of it."

One of my manager's subordinates missed a day of work and did not offer an explanation. He called her in and then reported the conversation to me, thus:

"I might have expected some word," he suggested.

"I tried to get back from up north last night," she said. "I was visiting family."

"That's nice. And you couldn't get back?"

"I thought there was a late train."

"And there wasn't?"

"No, in fact I was stranded for a while at the station."

"That's too bad. What did you do then?"

"I asked my brother-in-law if he could drive me."

"And he couldn't?"

She shook her head. "He had to get up at five to go to work, so he really couldn't."

"So then what did you do?"

"I prayed."

"Good idea. And?"

"I asked everybody else I knew who might be able to take me. No one was available, so I decided God didn't want me to come to work until today."

"You know what?" he said. "I think you had a fair, not a good but a fair, excuse for not getting back last night. It was your fault. You didn't check on the trains until it was too late. You tried hard to get a ride, which is commendable, and you prayed, which was also good. But to decide that because God didn't choose to rescue you after you had blundered is really not acceptable."

"What else could I have done?"

"At least you could have called me and told me your predicament."

"But it wasn't my fault. I—"

"I commend you," he said, "on trying to fix a frustrating situation. But saying it isn't your fault is wrong."

"It wasn't anybody's fault. It was just one of those things."

My manager told his worker that had she simply admitted her responsibility, he would have retroactively given her the day off and urged her to do better next time and to at least call him to let him know. Short of that, she should have at least been waiting at his office door to tell him her story when he arrived.

She not only had taken no responsibility, but she had also assumed that because she didn't feel at fault, she owed no one an explanation. She was outraged when he informed her that she would not be paid for the day she missed.

From that point on, her problems were his fault. She did not last long and last I heard is in her third job since.

One of my favorite examples of passing the blame, if one can have favorites of such irritating traits, is one in which the fault is transferred while the misdeed is ignored. One of you will recognize this scenario.

The teacher hassled you for goofing off. When she had to remind you again, she issued a detention. The explanation you gave us was that since she had not told you in advance that you would get a detention in lieu of a second warning, it wasn't fair.

"But were you goofing off?"

"Yeah, but if I had known how serious she was—"

"Then who's fault was it that you sat in detention and missed your ride?"

"Hers because she didn't tell me what would happen if—"

I once had a boss who was amused by non-excuse excuses. "I'm not even given excuses," he would lament. "I'm given reasons, as if that explains it. If I ask why third quarter profits are down, I'm told that we didn't expect the postal increase. No one tells me what's going to be done about it, why we weren't aware of it, how we will make up for it. Just reasons! Because *that* happened, our numbers don't work. I guess I'm supposed to feel good because, if it hadn't been for something unforeseen, we would have done swimmingly."

Needless to say, it wasn't enough. He wanted someone to take responsibility for failure and explain how it would be rectified.

In most cases, at least with me, blame shifting was really lying. I may have told myself it wasn't, but when I think back and really study the individual cases, I was pretending to be a victim of someone else's foul-up.

Oh, they may have really messed up, and I may truly have been a victim. But the responsibility had been mine, and thus I should have foreseen problems or been prepared to deal with them. Rather than rectify a situation, I claimed the alibi of someone else's failure and focused the attention there. I didn't sleep as well as I do now.

I wish I could remember the first time I simply took the blame, admitted my mistake, and set about righting it. I do recall that I began to be looked at differently by my superiors. They saw me as a responsible person, honest, eager to do things right. I didn't waste time trying to assess blame and point fingers. I even took some blame that probably wasn't mine. I knew if I studied the problem long enough I could find a place where I had let down, quit staying on top of something, and could have had something to do with the failure.

Take the blame, fix the problem, and live with a clear conscience.

At a high level meeting of VIPs it was the responsibility of a friend of mine to ask the proper department to provide a mobile rack for the people's coats. He sent through the paperwork, received a signed receipt, noted that the proper date and location were designated, and relaxed. On the night of the meeting he greeted the VIPs, introduced his boss for a brief introduction, and slipped out to be sure the dining room and meal were ready and the coat rack in place.

When he got downstairs he walked past where the rack should have been, checked with the food service staff, and found all that in order. He then shot a double take at the empty space by the wall. No rack. And here came footsteps on the stairs.

He ran to the department that was supposed to have provided the rack. The area was dark. He peered through the glass, shielding outside light with his hands. Three coat racks were available behind the locked door. He hollered for a maintenance man, and one appeared at the end of the hall, looking at him, puzzled.

"I need to get in here," he shouted.

"I can't let you do that," the man said.

"You have a master key, don't you?"

"Yes sir, but I can't—"

My friend ran toward him. They knew each other, so there was no threat. "The president needs a coat rack for the VIPs, and it's my responsibility."

"Did you requisition one?"

"Of course, but—"

"Then you did your job. Somebody else messed up."

"I'm not interested in that. Open this door, and I'll take the heat."

"I'll let you unlock it, but I'm not going to."

"Fair enough," my friend said, bouncing on his toes to get the maintenance man to hurry. Seconds later he was flying down the hall toward the dining room, pushing the rack ahead of him.

He whirled into sight just as the VIPs arrived. He stopped, took a deep breath, and tucked in his shirt. "Right here, folks," he said, gliding into position. "May I take your coats?"

The president never noticed how close they came to having a little faux pas. My friend's excuses and an explanation of how he had done his part would have been totally irrelevant. Paper trails don't cut it. He had been given the responsibility to provide the coat rack, and he had done it. Had he not done it, it would have been his fault. Someone else let him down, but he would have had to take the full blame.

I would love to be able to tell you that the department in charge apologized to him for the inconvenience, but —you guessed it—a shifting of the blame began. There had been an emergency, a new employee, an earlier quitting time, a misunderstanding.

Don't do that, guys. If you're asked to do something and you're counting on six other suppliers to make it happen, take responsibility. See that it gets done. Stay on top of it. People don't want excuses. They want performance.

And when something does go wrong, even if it's not your fault, express sorrow for the inconvenience, and make it right. Too often you could have done something to prevent the problem, so accept the blame too.

Accept responsibility for your own actions.

WATCH
YOUR
TONGUE

7

WATCH YOUR TONGUE

I hesitate to share this story, because it will make you crazy wondering who I am talking about, and that's not fair because I'm not going to tell you. If I did, I would be violating the very truth I want to promote here: watch your mouth. Guard your tongue.

Here's the story anyway. I'm sorry about the secret I must keep.

I was once honored to be invited to lunch by a big name. Author. Preacher. Evangelical leader. A known man. A godly man. I will not retract any of those descriptions despite my ensuing disappointment.

But suffice it to say that once the pleasantries were out of the way and we had talked some book business, this man proceeded to bad-mouth, criticize, gossip about, and harpoon his contemporaries. This one wasn't bright. That one was too harsh. This one had written the same book several times. That one had an unruly child. This one didn't study enough. One was too deep, another too shallow.

It was a classic case of a man not satisfied to be numbered among the few very best in his field. He had to rip the others to elevate himself. It was a shattering experience. He didn't even seem to notice that I had lost my appetite and my interest in conversing (two monumental rarities in my life, as you well know).

I didn't know what to make of it. I knew he had had some physical ailments. Perhaps they contributed. The best I could do was to chalk it off as a blind spot. I have mine, and God still uses and blesses me. There's no sense in expecting that man to be perfect either.

It wasn't long after that, however, that I heard him speak on the tongue in the book of James. Here were some of the texts he used:

> If anyone among you thinks he is religious, and does not bridle his tongue but deceives his own heart, this one's religion is useless (1:26).

> Even so the tongue is a little member and boasts great things. See how great a forest a little fire kindles! And the tongue is a fire, a world of iniquity. The tongue is so set among our members that it defiles the whole body, and sets on fire the course of nature; and it is set on fire by hell (3:5-6).

> But no man can tame the tongue. It is an unruly evil, full of deadly poison (3:8).

You can imagine the impact those verses had on me after having heard him disobey them. He intoned such things as, "We must not use our tongues to injure one another. We must not gossip and backbite."

I was too young and intimidated to confront the man. What might he have said? Who was I to correct him? Had I not been just as guilty within my own family and circle? I felt self-righteous that I would not bad-mouth someone to another outside my immediate confidants, but then I began to feel bad about that too.

When is talking about someone acceptable? When we precede it by asking for prayer for them? That's one of the oldest gossip justifiers in the business. "Well, we need to really pray for her, because I understand their love life was horrible too."

"Oh, really? I would want to pray intelligently. So, like what?"

There are times when a board or someone's superiors must talk about a person. Even that, if you have made it a practice not to talk about people when they are not around, can make you feel uncomfortable. When it has to be done for the protection of others or for the integrity of a ministry, I believe there should still be guidelines and bounds. Nothing should be said that could just as easily not be said. If details must be known, they should be shared in humility and full confidentiality.

How about gossiping within the family? We trust each other. We can keep confidences. Who else will ever know? Do you know what she did? What she said? Where he's going? What happened to him? That's dangerous talk.

There is little I keep from your mother, but when I do it's because I don't want to injure her view of another. Sometimes I have to correct her view of someone so that she doesn't get hurt or used. That is difficult and painful, but occasionally it's necessary.

What's wrong with gossip? Why do I urge you to guard your tongues, when talking about other people is so much fun?

In my opinion, gossip accomplishes four things, all of them bad:

It hurts the reputation of the person being spoken about.

It affects the impression of that person by the hearer of the gossip.

It lowers the reputation of the teller, which is precisely the opposite of what he intended.

And it violates Scripture (see above).

Let me be clear. Gossip is not necessarily made up of falsehoods. In fact, if gossip is untrue, it is probably less harmful to the target than true stories would be. If a rumor is false, time will reveal it. If gossip is true, time will reveal that too. Don't defend gossip by saying that you know it to be fact. It's still damaging information about someone that does not need to be shared, unless for someone else's protection.

For instance, if your best friend said her daughter had been befriended by an adult you knew to have a background of sex offenses, clearly it would be your duty to inform your friend. It would not be your duty to tell everyone in town. Perhaps the man has changed and is doing well. It's important for him to be careful and for people around him to be cautious, but it is not necessary to besmirch a reputation by telling everyone the truth from the past.

The ability to keep confidences need be violated only once to ruin your reputation. At your tender ages you have already suffered from this heartbreak. You told the one person you could trust your deepest, darkest secret.

And now everybody knows. It was a secret, so everyone found out one at a time, but each one told one, and no one expected anyone to tell anyone else.

Now it's common knowledge. It's been said that the best secrets are kept between two best friends when one of them is dead. It's also been said that truth and time walk hand in hand, so untruths spoken about you will eventually be exposed.

What are we to do in the face of gossip? My mother says she doesn't remember this, but I have a vivid memory from my early childhood (in fact, in our first house) of her pulling out the vacuum cleaner and sweeping while a neighborhood gossip tried to keep her attention. The woman finally got the message and marched off.

I've seen my father quietly walk away from dirty jokes and gossip-filled conversations. I have an uncle who will respond to any bad comment about anyone with something good.

"That guy is really a creep."

"He sure seems a good family man. I've always liked him."

He even turns complaints around. Once I lamented about a friend who had had to take a humiliatingly modest position after having been forced out of a job in a mass mid-management cut-back.

"I'll bet he's thrilled to have an income right now," my uncle said. "It's a good break for him while he gets back on his feet."

I once was lied about in a most despicable manner. The woman who spread the story told it with just enough nuances and imitations of my speech and mannerisms that no one who heard it had any reason to believe it wasn't so.

I have always taken pride in the fact that I do not major on the minors. I have many friends who do not share my faith, and I enjoy showing them that I accept them and love them. I would no more criticize someone for smoking or drinking or doing something else that I consider off-limits to me than I would tell them I was better than they because I was a Christian. My posture is that I am a sinner like anyone else and that Christ has saved me.

When He has done His saving work in their lives, He will deal with them about personal habits and lifestyle. Expecting an unbeliever to have biblical values is a form of condescension at odds with true Christianity.

That's why, when I was working in a setting with both believers and non-believers, I went to lunch with many who smoked and even drank. They knew where I stood and didn't try to get me to do the same.

But one day one of the guys began acting funny around me. He took his ashtray and put it on his other side. "I wouldn't want you to have to breathe any of my smoke," he said.

I had never said anything about that, and wouldn't have. I smiled. He didn't.

The next day he said something else about smoking in front of me. "I suppose you're going to slap my hand if I light up again."

I squinted at him. "What are you taking about?"

"Oh, we all know what you said to Pam."

I wasn't playing dumb. I was dumb. I had no idea what he was referring to. Pam was the receptionist. I had not had three conversations with her in a month, and those were only to ask about her family. I never said anything about her smoking or looked askance at her because of it.

It took me several days to pull from my friend what I was supposed to have said to Pam. She had fabricated a running debate we were supposed to be having—how I would slap her hand lightly every time I saw her with a cigarette. I would move the ashtray, cough aloud, make a joke, ask her how she could put such filthy things in her mouth.

This friend, I'll call him Bob, came to believe me. I said, "Bob, have you *ever* known me to be like that or talk like that about anything to anyone?"

He admitted he had not. I wondered if it could have been a case of mistaken identity, but there were only a dozen of us working in that office and no one looked like me. Where was she getting this, and how long had everyone else been thinking what a clod I was?

Months.

Finally I knew I had to confront her. Someone must have tipped her off. She quit in the middle of one afternoon, and I was unable to even track her down by phone. I reached her father, who told me he didn't know where she was. I left my number and name, and he said, "Oh, you're the goody two shoes who ran her out of there because she smokes."

I know it could have been worse. She could have accused me of immorality or harassment or whatever. There was some good that came of it, however. Painful as it was, it allowed me to know the feeling of what Scripture calls being falsely accused.

"Blessed are you when they revile and persecute you, and say all kinds of evil against you falsely for My sake" (Matthew 5:11).

What made that experience so difficult was that I could think of no reason whatever that Pam would even hold animosity for me, let alone that she would concoct such a story. It was terribly frustrating for months, trying to reach her. I even wrote her, but never heard from her again.

I felt a terrible need to vindicate myself and had to work at not talking about it constantly. I was sure that if my other friends thought I was protesting too loudly I would appear guilty. It was such a minor thing in their minds that they couldn't understand why I was so eager to defend myself.

It reminds me of your story, Dallas, when you were in your friend's room as a child and he climbed on the dresser and tipped it over. When his mother burst into the room, he blamed it on you. And she spanked you for it! How could you deny it? A guilty person would have done the same.

The tongue can be so evil, but it can also do such good. How else would we tell you we love you? How else would we encourage you and praise you and exhort you? Sure, that can be done on paper, but if my loved ones ever lost their ability to speak, I would most miss their familiar voices saying things I love to hear.

I love to talk with your mother because she's always had a beautiful speaking voice. I love to hear you boys laugh and tell your stories and especially tell each other that you love one another.

I want you to always remember the potency of the tongue.

Watch it. Guard it. Keep it. And use it for good.

You'll be interested to know that Bob eventually became a Christian.

WORK
BEFORE
YOU
PLAY,
BUT
PLAY!

8

WORK BEFORE YOU PLAY, BUT PLAY!

I've told this story in other venues, and even in another book, but it helps me make this point, so forgive me and bear with me as I quickly summarize it.

Before we had children I worked for a publishing company where it was my job to interview people for first-person stories. In a brief period, say a couple of months, I happened to interview five men whose children were grown. I was talking to each about something different. With one it was his testimony, with another his business, with another an interesting anecdote, and so on. But with each I got to the point where I asked if he had any regrets.

They all had that in common. It was almost as if they had conspired to send me a message. Each said he wished he'd spent more time with his family. None of them had kids who went off the deep end or were away from the Lord in serious rebellion. The fathers simply wished they had spent more time with their children.

Your mother and I discussed it at length and made a decision. Though we wouldn't be having children for a couple more years, we set a policy. From the time I got home from work until the time the kids went to bed, I would not do any writing or any work from the office.

That allowed for some interesting bonding between me and you boys as babies. I gave baths, changed diapers, spoon fed, crawled, wrestled, ran, and did all those things babies and toddlers do. I saved my free-lance writing for late at night and usually had between two and three hours each day with you.

I was there when you said your first words, took your first steps, prayed to receive Christ, and began to really grow, physically and spiritually. I wouldn't trade it for anything. I especially enjoyed being there, Dallas—though you didn't know I could hear you—when you told your action figure, "If you die in this mission and go to heaven, you can ask Jesus for anything you want, and if it's all right with your mom, He'll give it you."

Frequently I encourage fathers to spend more time with their kids. My nearly three hours a day with you guys remains a precious thing to me, even if you have grown tired of it, or of me.

You have commented on the uniqueness of how we play and romp and have so much fun, whether it's just running into town for a burger, playing baseball or basketball or football, or having snowball fights, building snow forts, whatever. Since very few dads seem to do that, the

other kids in the neighborhood come to our place for the
novelty of it. They've never "shot" someone my size and
seen him tumble through a snowbank to his temporary
death. Or been tackled by someone my size either.

We've had fun, and we always will. All that to say
this: I want you to remember to work before you play, but
be sure to play.

I know it's probably some vestige of a Protestant
work ethic that always makes me require you guys to do
your homework and your chores before we watch a game
on TV or play in the yard or do anything fun. But it also
pays off. I use such things myself as rewards for getting a
chapter done, a book read, a project finished for Mom.

You complain and badger and wonder why we can't
play now if you promise, promise, promise to do the other
stuff later. Maybe when you're grown or almost grown
you'll try it your way. You'll put off the tough stuff to enjoy the moment, but you'll discover what I've discovered:

A game of touch football is not as much fun when
you keep recalling that you still have to rake those leaves
or clean the garage or do the dishes. Doing chores, on the
other hand, is not so bad when you can look forward to
some fun. When I commuted every day to and from Chicago, I motivated myself to get my work done by thinking
of the payoff: playing with you guys, having dinner with
the family, doing things together, laughing, surprising
people. Your friends can't believe it when an adult acts
crazy, but they keep coming back, don't they?

I know you feel put upon when I'm rigid on this and
you can't watch the Bears or the Cubs or the Bulls until
that homework is completely done. And no, I can't think
of a reason it would be so bad if you watched now and
worked later—except that it works better this way. Work
before you play.

Psychologists say a sign of good mental health is delaying gratification. In other words, we are born wanting what we want when we want it. We scream for milk, we scream for attention, we scream for toys, we scream to be changed. When we get that bottle, we empty it right now, and if it's not enough, we scream for more.

There's no thought, no wondering if maybe this is the last bottle of milk on earth. We don't hoard it, sip it, protect it. We go for it. When we're pre-schoolers and we get a cupcake, what do we do with it? Do we eat the slightly dryer cake and save the frosting for the last few bites? No, we lick that tasty stuff right off the top and then lose interest in the dry cake.

When we're at the pizza place and they bring out a pitcher of pop, do we save it to enjoy with the pie? Adults usually do. Kids don't. As long as they have any, they feel they have plenty. But if Mom and Dad won't invest in some more, they don't enjoy their meal as much.

What do we do with our money? Do we save and plan, or do we spend the first bundle we accumulate? That will lead to credit woes in adulthood, so beware. Delay gratification. The longer you put it off and anticipate it, the better.

In fact, sometimes the anticipation is better than the payoff. Remember our big family trip last year? Thinking about it and planning it and especially talking about it were as much fun as the trip itself. And the trip was great. It simply never could have lived up to our dreams.

Now that I work at home full time, I use this work-before-play policy more than ever. There are so many fun things to do around the house, especially in the summer when you're all home, but unless I discipline myself, I won't get my work done. I look forward to a good chat with Mom, but I don't allow myself that luxury until I've reached a certain place in my work mid-morning. Then there's the paper, and the mail, and lunch. But I have to reach certain goals before I break for each one.

During the school year I know when you guys will be home, so I charge headlong toward that time, setting myself an ambitious goal of pages written, edited, printed out. If you have a game, or if I'm picking you up after practice, I force myself to accomplish more before that time. It's so much better to be writing while looking forward to some fun than to watch a game knowing I have to be back at the keyboard in the dead of night while you're asleep.

This delaying of gratification is more than just a maturing device that makes life more fun. It can also keep you pure. As you grow up and find your life's mate, you will begin to look forward to your wedding night and honeymoon with great anticipation, eager to consummate your love and make your union real. The percentage of couples who save that glorious time of discovery and most personal gift-giving is shrinking annually. If you have learned well the value of delayed gratification, you have a better chance at waiting until God's time.

I once read a wonderful allegory about this. A group of friends decided to have a reunion at their favorite steak place. They hadn't seen each other since all left for different colleges. When they met in the parking lot of the restaurant, they introduced spouses and fiancees to one another and giggled about how they had not eaten since breakfast so they could enjoy the thick, juicy, mouthwatering beef with all the trimmings. They lingered by the front door of the place, lusting after the menu and deciding what they would have with their steaks.

They thought of previous trips to this place and what fun they had had sating their appetites and enjoying each other. But when they reached for the door they realized the place was not open yet. They were an hour early.

That was good, they decided. They would be only hungrier and would enjoy the wonderful meal that much more. They hung around the parking lot trying to keep their minds off their hunger, but that menu kept drawing them back.

One of the young women was almost faint from hunger. She sent her boyfriend to the fast-food place across the street to get her some fries to tide her over. While there he remembered how he loved those fast-food shakes, but he didn't want to look selfish. He returned with several shakes and several orders of fries. All that served to do was trigger the hunger pangs, and soon others were sent for just one burger—no, a double; yeah, me too.

When the steak place opened, the group slowly filed in and were led to their special table. They had a long-standing reservation, and the management wanted to make the night special for them. They all ordered their steaks, but no one was really hungry anymore. The best part of the evening had been ruined by their inability to delay gratification.

Three Christmas stories illustrate my own coming to terms with this truth. One year I bought my two older brothers such great gifts that I just had to give them a sneak preview before they were wrapped. That spoiled the fun for them and for me.

The next Christmas I was home alone one evening with all the packages under the tree. One package, from my eldest brother, looked easy to unwrap and re-wrap. And so I did. The present was a couple of pairs of sports socks I really wanted. It was a good gift, but now I had ruined the fun. I had such a highly developed conscience at that age that I was forced to confess to my brother my sneakery before I could sleep that night. He couldn't imagine what the big deal was over a couple of lousy pairs of socks. He forgave me, and I thought he was the greatest.

Then came the Christmas where I just knew my mother was going to buy me a big, warm parka. I needed one, wanted one, and had even tried a few on. That over-stuffed suit box under the tree had to be my coat.

I was maturing. I restrained myself. A few times I hefted and shook the box. It was the right weight and feel, no rattling, good bulk. Sure I might rather have had a train set, but I was looking forward to this coat. We seldom had extra money, but Mom sure knew how to buy the necessities. She wouldn't scrimp on a good winter coat.

I began referring to the gift as my coat, and Mom never blinked. "If you want to think it's a coat," she teased, "that's all right."

"But isn't it?"

"I'm not saying. It's a present. A surprise. Don't ask."

"Can I save my coat to open last?"

She nodded. It had to be my coat.

When the big day came we all opened everything except that coat. The second to last gift was a certificate for my brother so he could buy his first sport coat, sometime after Christmas. Now it was time for the biggie: my coat.

I tore off the wrapping, sliced through the tape, dug out the paper wrapping, all the while imagining myself in that warm wrap. But it wasn't a coat at all. It wasn't a toy. It was books! The first nine or ten volumes of the *Golden Book Encyclopedia.*

What a hit! I had not even dreamed of so valuable a gift. It was a treasure. Mom explained that every week at the grocery store she would pick up one more volume until eventually I had all twenty or so. I devoured those books. An encyclopedia a kid could understand! I read every page as the volumes arrived.

What a loss that would have been if I had peeked! It remains one of the best gifts I have ever received. (Eventually I got that coat, and last year my mother gave me the train set I always wanted. You guys played with it almost as much as I did.)

I don't want to leave this subject without returning to the emphasis on the payoff. Remember, I'm saying work before you play, but I'm also reminding you to make sure you play. Some people work so hard and long they don't leave time to play. I'm kind of an oldish, broken down forty-one now, but in my mind I'm still a child (you won't get an argument from anyone on that!). I think it's because I still make time, not just take it—make it—to have fun every day.

That's why our house is full of laughter and pranks and jokes and silliness. We all have lots of hard work to do, especially Mom (see next chapter). You guys are good students, and we want that to continue. I have things to write that have to be on time and, I hope, effective. So we work. And we work before we play. But we do play.

So, don't forget to get your work done first so that you can enjoy playing all the more. And always remember to play. You owe it to yourself. It's a reward for getting your work done.

WOMEN
WORK
HARDER
THAN
MEN

9

WOMEN WORK HARDER THAN MEN

We're going to jump right into this one, boys, and the only reason I didn't put this earlier in the book is that I didn't want to alienate half the readership right off the bat.

Ready?

Women work harder than men.

I'm not saying that's the way it should be or that that's the way it always is, but this is a truism from my perspective. Now, you'll have your manual laborers saying, "No woman could cut down trees eight hours a day," or, "No woman could unload a moving van from dawn to dusk five days a week."

OK, but I'd like to see any one of those guys do what a mother of pre-schoolers does everyday. It may not be like chopping trees or lifting heavy furniture, but it is also relentless, frustrating, and never-ending. The old adage is: Man may work from sun to sun, but woman's work is never done.

The stereotypical white collar man has such weighty responsibilities that when he gets home he must relax while everyone waits on him—including the wife and the dog—or he must retreat to his den to putz around, read the paper, or snooze. Or he may be the type who must immediately change clothes and spend the time before dinner using his hands in his workshop, shifting his thinking to another side of the brain to relax.

Blue collar workers have more justification for crashing when they get home. The stereotype here is a man flopping into his easy chair for a night of television.

In either scenario you see a woman in the background. The way the modern picture has changed, the woman is probably working full-time too. Either way, regardless what the man does all day, he takes breaks. Coffee breaks morning and afternoon, lunch breaks mid-day. If the woman works, she gets those breaks too, but often she must use them to get grocery shopping or other errands done. Because when she gets home, Big and Ugly needs catering.

I hate stereotypes, and I usually tune out when someone begins a sentence with "Well, men like this . . ." or "Men think that . . ," because generalizations are usually insulting even if true. I've heard marriage experts talk about men being insensitive and logical and practical while women are supposed to be emotional and eager to share their feelings. Maybe that's true, but maybe many men possess feminine sides to their personalities too, without any proclivity for sexual confusion.

My dad is not a talkative person, but he can be emotional and sensitive. Housework was never beneath him and neither was taking care of babies, which my older brothers and I saw when our ten-years-later tagalong appeared. Here was dad, a police executive and ex-Marine, doing whatever had to be done to keep the house running while Mom recuperated.

Dad cooked meals, scrubbed floors, did laundry, washed dishes, changed the baby, and taught his ten-, twelve-, and thirteen-year-olds to do the same. I get a kick out of hearing about husbands who have never changed a dirty diaper or washed a load of clothes. It may be nothing to brag about, but I'll bet my brothers have done as much of that as I have.

You'll do it too, if you plan to be fair and sensitive husbands. The day is long past where you can expect your wife to do typical "woman's work" alone. If your mother worked outside the home, I would no more expect her to continue to have full responsibility for the running of the house than I would expect her to do my work.

I have been fortunate, and you have been unusually blessed, that your mother has not had to work since the first baby arrived. You have an unusual mom, as you well know. Only when you've been married several years will you realize even part of the scope of her responsibilities and uniqueness. One thing I am always quick to brag about, and really must stop (maybe by putting it in print once and for all I can give it a rest), is that in more than twenty years of marriage, you mother has been sick for an entire day only once.

I credit her robust upbringing on a farm in central Illinois, her work ethic, her sense of responsibility, and maybe her ability to cover when she really should have stayed in bed. But she's industrious, a worker, a woman not afraid to get her hands dirty and her muscles sore. People who see her only at church or in dress-up situations would be shocked to know that this beautiful woman works in the soil, takes her end of a heavy piece of furniture from the van to the house, brings in firewood when necessary, and is anything but a dainty weakling.

There has been the occasional migraine or touch of flu that has kept her down for a few hours, but she didn't even let a finger smashed on a window sill or a broken toe slow her. And only once did a stomach virus take her out of commission for a whole day.

So, why am I saying women work harder than men, and how do I know? Because my father was never so exhausted as when he was doing work my mother typically did. And when your mother is away on a women's retreat or a conference, I am left to do her typical chores. Take it from me, boys, I speak the truth.

There's something bigger about a woman's responsibility than simply the sum of the jobs. When I do the dishes or shop for groceries or give a kid a bath and put him to bed, it's no big deal. It's just something added to what I normally do. But when she's not here and I have to do that along with everything else, it's overwhelming. And it is a twenty-four-hour-a-day proposition.

There also must be little sense of accomplishment outside of a few compliments from the family—and for too many women, those are few and far between. Dishes are washed to be used again. Clothes are washed to be dirtied again. Sweeping, dusting, mopping, are all temporary stopgap measures.

If a woman is working outside the home, she might be involved in projects that are eventually finished and have accomplished something. At home her work is repetitious and frustrating and boring and too often unappreciated. It's only her raising of children—which must be a

shared responsibility—that is one day finished and hope-
fully permanent.

I know feminists would demand to know why I consider household duties women's work, and, I repeat, if
your wife also works outside the home, you have every bit
as much responsibility for domestic chores as she does.
Whether her position is as "important" or "crucial" or as
highly compensated as yours, it's not fair that one of you
should have, in essence, two full-time jobs.

My admonition to you is to try to manage your situation in such a way that your wife does not have to work
outside the home after you've had children. I know I'm
considered old-fashioned, out of date, and out of touch on
this issue, but if a woman wants to work because raising
her children is not challenging enough, then she should
put off having children. I don't want to get into argu-
ments. I could do a whole book on how much more re-
warding and important child-rearing is than finding one's
self in a challenging career.

I sympathize with those women who really must work,
and I share their frustration with those who think that
only a man can achieve anything in this world. But back to
my point.

Because of insensitive men, women who work outside the home often have to d⌐ all the work at home too,
which is unfair and clearly supports my view that women
work harder than men. But in my opinion even those
women who are full-time homemakers work harder than
men.

I have had to do this work at times, and I'll take man-
aging, writing, editing, even manual laboring any day.
The around-the-clock responsibility is too stressful and
must, to many women, feel like jail.

I don't tell you that women work harder than men
just to impress you with my sensitivity or to try to make

friends of those women readers who haven't already written me off as a male chauvinist pig. I tell you so that you will not allow it to be so in your own home, now or when you are on your own.

I am aware that you can count on the fingers of one hand the homes in which the kids are expected to wash their own clothes. You'll thank us for that some day. And I have been surprised that what I thought was an evangelical tradition—the kids taking turns clearing the table, washing, and drying the dishes—is also a unique bit of torture we inflict upon you. Other kids get to watch TV without asking, don't they? Trust me, this is not terminal.

To your delight, you may find that your wife does not want you to do the work. She may want help only once in a while, to be spelled occasionally, to be appreciated a lot, to be frequently reminded that you realize how important and crucial and difficult her work is.

It is so easy to take in stride what Mom does for us every day that we need to constantly remind ourselves. You know what this place looks like when she's away for a few days. I know she has a better scheme; she stays ahead of the big work. Rather than let dishes pile up or messes grow in the family room, she tidies up constantly—or reminds us to. She's so regular in it that we hardly notice until she's gone. Without her there to remind us, our empty glasses and our empty pop cans and our used bowls sit in the family room overnight, and within a couple of days we have to bring in the front-end loader and get to work.

I could spend another entire chapter just listing the things your mother does every day that we would find irritating to have to do ourselves. Develop sensitivity. Offer to help. Find out what she likes to do least, and do it for her once in a while.

As earthy and industrious as your mom is, you know by now that one thing she has never been able to stomach are sick kids in the night. She is up so early and works out-doors enough that she is one who needs an early bedtime. Because of that and her natural aversion to the sights and smells that go along with a six-year-old with stomach flu, I have unofficially taken charge of such duties.

I'm not boasting. Please. This is no fun chore for me either. To be aroused from a sound sleep to a crying, em-barrassed, ill, messy, smelly child is not on my list of fa-vorite things. But there is a sense of satisfaction in getting kid and bed cleaned up and tucked in, and I have loved as-suring you boys that I'm glad to be able to help when you feel your worst and most vulnerable. I know what it's like to be a problem for your parents in the middle of the night and all the emotions that go with that.

I share that to encourage you to find those few things that would really make your wife's job easier and volun-teer to do them. It's only a token of thanks and a small ef-fort to lighten her load. Keep her happy, guys. No matter what anybody says, her work will always be harder than yours.

PLAY
TO
YOUR
STRENGTHS

10

PLAY TO YOUR STRENGTHS

Does Larry Bird work on his speed?

Does he work on his jumping?

Does he work on his physique?

Man, the best white player in the history of professional basketball has three weaknesses there. I mean, he's slow. He can't jump but a few inches off the ground. His body looks softer than it probably is, but he could be stronger.

The guy is legendary not just because of his incredible stamina and shooting skills, but because of his great passing and court knowledge. He seems to have eyes in the back of his head and can hit the open man without looking at him.

The answer is no. Though Larry Bird has been known as the most dedicated and hard-working professional in decades, going to the arena in the mid-afternoon to get in a couple of hours' worth of shooting every day, he does not work on the three weaknesses above. He's six-feet-nine, so with a better leap he might be able to play in the stratosphere with the great leapers. With more speed he could lead breakaways and be even tougher on defense. And with some weight work, he could hone that chalky body into something worth looking at.

So what does he work at during those two extra hours most multimillionaires spend doing nothing or finding more ways to make money? He shoots and works on his endurance.

He's already one of the best shooters in history, a big man who won the three-point shooting contest two years running and who has an assortment of shots with either hand that would put a Globetrotter to shame. And until he began to have foot troubles later in his career, he was a workhorse, logging as many minutes per night as anyone in the game.

Getting my drift? Bird is not going to get much faster. He's not going to ever jump much higher. And his body is never going to look like Michael Jordan's. He plays to his strengths, polishes them, makes them unbeatable.

How do you suppose it makes the competition feel to know that the best shooter in basketball is already at the arena, hours before the game, shooting? They'll be all over him in the game, cutting him off, trying to shut him down, making him shoot over gigantic young leapers. They'll try to deny him the ball, then deny him the lane. They'll bump him, hold him, push him, try to frustrate him. They'll

foul him too, but of course he's one of the highest percentage foul shooters since Rick Barry.

He doesn't concentrate on his weaknesses. He con-
centrates on what has made him who he is, and all it has
done has made him better. He's in the twilight of his career now and may have only a few seasons left. But when
he has an inch, he'll make a basket. When they close off
the middle, he'll hit from the outside. When they take
away his right hand, he'll shoot with the left, inside, outside, and from the top of the key. And if they somehow
succeed in taking away his shot, he'll hit the open man
with a perfect pass.

In his workout he'll never quit running. He may move
right and left and straight to the hoop, getting his own re-
bounds, but never slowing down. He likes to see if he can
make a hundred shots in a row from all over the court,
never stopping to wipe the sweat pouring from his head to
his chin to his shirt. If anyone else did that on game day,
he'd have nothing left for the game.

What it gives Bird is confidence. No matter where he
is on the court or who's on him or what the situation is, he
has confidence that when he goes up for the shot, it will
merely be his thousandth or so of the day. Odds are it will
go in.

Want to learn something from Larry Bird? Don't rest
on your laurels. Never be satisfied with being great. Don't
ever think you've arrived. Never stop practicing. And most
of all, and the point of this chapter, forget your weaknesses. Play to your strengths.

Now, of course, there are some weaknesses that have
to be worked on and overcome. For instance, if Bird were
six-three instead of six-nine, he would not get away with a
lack of speed or jumping ability. It takes years to improve
on those, but he would have to invest the time to make the
grade.

Walter Payton, one of the strongest runners in the history of the National Football League, was not a tall man. He couldn't do anything about that. In fact, had he been taller, he might rather have been a basketball player. Basketball was his favorite sport in high school. He was not short at five-ten, but neither was he tall enough for major college basketball or for seeing over the line to be a great quarterback. He could throw the ball as far as any QB, but his size was a handicap in the backfield.

His strengths were speed and musculature and endurance, and he had an uncanny ability to stay upright even when being hit at full speed by defenders. The latter was a trick no one else ever seemed to catch onto. As he was moving down the field and could see that someone had the right angle on him and was about to hurl himself into Payton, Walter would skip a step on purpose, throwing himself into the defender, catching him completely off balance and reeling. In fact, if the defender simply stopped and refused to hit Payton, Walter would have gone sprawling.

But even after more than a decade in the NFL, no defenders had caught onto this trick. They would dutifully lower their shoulder into the superstar, knocking him upright and usually sending him on his way.

You had to see a Payton workout to believe it. Here was another man who ignored his weaknesses and honed his strengths. He used to like to insist (though with a twinkle) that he never worked out with weights. Indeed, he rarely did in anyone else's presence.

But I once saw the weights in his house. If he bench-pressed what was on the bar, he would have been at world class level for his weight. Anyone who ever saw him in only a pair of shorts wouldn't find that hard to believe. He weighed just a few pounds over 200, probably never more than 210, yet he was as massively muscled and sculptured as any athlete I've ever seen. His skin was drawn so tight across his biceps that it appeared his muscle would break the skin if he flexed. His ankles were thin as a thoroughbred's, his calves as big around as a lineman's. His wrists were thick like Henry Aaron's (who was a bigger man), and his hands and fingers were bigger than those of men weighing 300 pounds.

What did Walter work on? Take a lesson. His strengths.

I never saw him run Suicide Hill in Mississippi, where he enjoyed running his contemporaries into the ground. The hill consisted of rock and cinder and dirt and seemed to go straight up. He would tell visiting teammates that he worked out "up there."

"How do you get up there?" they'd ask.

"I'll race you," he'd say.

"You don't drive a four-wheeler up there?"

"No need." And he'd take off running, digging, charging, slipping, sliding, pushing straight up. A few seconds later he would see the challenger starting out, falling, skinning, scraping himself, and getting up again.

"My two to your one," Walter would cackle.

"What?"

"I'll go up and down and back up before you get up there once!"

They'd wave him off derisively.

He'd beat them in a walk. He might do that several times a day during the off season. He would simply not allow himself to get out of shape. He came to training camp every year in playing form, ready to win the wind sprints and outlast everyone. Why? He played to his strengths.

His workouts in suburban Chicago were something else. He drove to a local high school and parked his car strategically in the grass near one end of the track. He would do pull-ups, push-ups, sit-ups, and other calisthenics to break a sweat—which is not easy when you're in the kind of shape he's in. (I once watched him paint one entire wall in about five minutes just because of his strength and agility. He didn't even breathe hard.)

Then he would begin his running, first a quarter or a half mile, hard. Then wind sprints while still recovering from the distance run. Then sprint a hundred, jog a hundred, sprint a hundred, walk a hundred, sprint a hundred, jog a hundred, and so on. He would keep this up, truly sprinting and working on every alternate hundred, until he was nearly unconscious. When he finished what felt to him like his last flying hundred, he would walk one more, and then begin an all-out quarter mile sprint.

We're talking about a mass of muscle here that is into oxygen debt and suffering. The muscles are throbbing and twitching, the face is contorted, the body is heaving itself around the track as fast as it can go. Even to a superstar like Walter that car seemed to get farther and farther away as he approached it. His vision would blur, his head pound, his lungs gasp, yet he forced his legs to pump. Any other athlete anywhere—I'm convinced even iron man tri-athletes—would have been run into the ground by then.

The last ten steps are unconscious. The body lurches and crumbles next to the car, and he lets it do its own recovery regardless how he lands. He's out, breathing heavily, sweating profusely, unable to move a muscle. He comes to in about twenty seconds.

Are you sitting down? He jogs another quarter mile before going home.

His explanation? He doesn't want to take anything for granted. He wants to fully work out every sinew, ligament, tendon, muscle, organ, and tissue. Trainers who saw him do that told him he was crazy, that he had overworked, that the last half of that workout was redundant and as harmful as it was helpful.

I'm not recommending that you use Walter Payton as a workout model. Unless you want to run for 275 yards in an NFL game or set a career rushing record that will never be broken. He played to his strengths, improved the qualities that got him where he wanted to go, and made himself better. He had one of the most unrealistic and yet interesting personal goals I've ever heard. Of course, he never achieved it and no one ever will.

He wanted to lead the NFL in rushing, total yardage, reception yardage, and touchdowns, be named MVP of the league and of the Pro Bowl, and then play so well the next season that he was named the Comeback Player of the Year.

Everyone who heard him say that thought it was a great joke. It would be like Michael Jordan, the year he started on the all-star team and was top scorer and best defensive player in the NBA, winning Comeback Player of the year the next season. It may have sounded funny, but Payton wasn't smiling. He took nothing for granted. He had not been blessed with height, and there was nothing he could do about that. What he could work on he worked on and made himself the best he could be, which also happened to make him the best there ever was.

Not all of my examples for this truth should come from the world of sports. I've heard a great preacher and seminary president say the same thing. He spent years, he said, on trying to shore up his weaknesses, to do a little better in all those areas in which he knew himself to be weak. Finally it dawned on him to concentrate on his strengths. It was freeing, he said. He began to enjoy his life and his ministry as never before. He delegated or ignored those things he wasn't cut out to do, and he concentrated on being a thinker and planner, a preacher and teacher and administrator.

Many of my colleagues and I have discovered this too late, so you may too. D.L. Moody preached this message: do one thing well, not many things in an average way. George Sweeting likens the man who spreads himself too thin to a Swiss army knife he had as a boy. "It did a dozen things," he says, "none of them particularly well."

There are many things I enjoy doing and wish I could say I do well. I'd love to be a good salesman, an outstanding speaker, a musician. I enjoy teaching and photography, and I think I'd even enjoy learning to fly an airplane. I greatly enjoyed management, and I think most people liked to work for me.

But I'm a writer. I may not even be the writer I'd like to think I am, but I believe this is my gift and my calling. And although I may still dabble in the things I listed above (sans the piloting, I'm afraid), this is where I have cast my lot. I want to say with others who have learned this lesson: This one thing I do . . .

Psychologist James Dobson says that having a specialty is a key to raising a healthy teenager. Excelling in at least one area will result in positive self-esteem.

Don't get me wrong. I admire those who can do it all. But there are only so many Bo Jacksons who can play two professional sports. Only so many Chuck Swindolls, who are as accomplished at writing as they are at speaking.

If you can be one of those modern day Ben Franklins, more power to you. In the meantime, I urge you to find your strength and play to it. The weaknesses, unless they are harmful to you or society, will take care of themselves.

Find your thing and go for it.

SOME
THINGS
ARE
BLACK
AND
WHITE

11

SOME THINGS *ARE* BLACK AND WHITE

Though you will discover as you grow older that life is not as tidy as you once thought, and that black-and-white issues tend to gray around the edges, don't make the mistake of assuming that nothing is absolute.

Some things *are* black and white.

You've heard the axiom "It Takes Two to Tango," or "There Are Always Two Sides to an Argument," or "There Are Exceptions to Every Rule."

Let me run down a few scenarios for you and see if you still buy into those "accepted truths."

I personally know of at least one divorce (the ultimate argument) where the wife was indeed an innocent and of-

fended party. I'm not saying she was perfect or even someone I would want to be married to. I am saying that the offending party, the adulterer, the deserter, the abuser, in
all his manic rages, never even accused his wife of anything remotely connected to justifiable grounds for divorce.

Again, hear me, I'm not saying—especially in this case
—that the wife was a model spouse. She may not have
even been a better than average wife. She was human. She
made mistakes. She was impatient at times, shrewish and
nagging at others, she admits. But not even her philander-
ing husband would say that she didn't love him in word
and deed. He couldn't say she had ever broken her marriage promise. She had never done anything but try to
keep a bad marriage together.

Now then, the black and white. The adulterer, the di-
vorcer, the leaver is the guilty party, the offending party,
the one in the wrong. The stayer, the worker, the promise-
keeper, the admittedly imperfect one who never gave up,
never quit loving and trying, and who fought the sunder-
ing legal action is innocent and offended.

I feel the need to make that clear because in this age
of rampant adultery and divorce, it becomes easier to ra-
tionalize these things.

"They weren't right for each other from the beginning."

"Well, she was no prize."

"No wonder he went looking for love somewhere
else."

And on and on.

Perhaps frustration was justified. Perhaps despair
was justified. Perhaps even a little self-pity and dreaming
how it might have been with someone else is understand-
able. But nothing justifies sexual sin. Nothing justifies
breaking promises, living lies.

Admittedly, in many bad marriages there are two sides. Both are unfaithful. Both are mean and nasty and abusive, lying, promise-breakers. Neither, however, may use the other's sins as justification for his own. And in those cases, yes, it takes two, there are two sides, and if we knew everything that went on behind closed doors, we wouldn't take sides.

Neither am I saying that it is always right for the offended party to stay. I happen to be among those who believe that the God who is the author of life and the antithesis of death does not "call" an abused spouse to remain in a life-threatening situation.

However, back to my point. Sometimes, things are black and white, and someone is guilty and someone is innocent. While it may usually, I repeat usually, be wisest not take sides, especially in the divorce of friends, there are times when you should learn all you can and cast your lot with the offended party.

That doesn't mean to be an enabler when a hurting person wants to vent and spew venom about a former spouse. But it does mean assuring that friend that she is a person of value, that she was treated unfairly, that her trust was trampled, but that she still has loyal friends.

Some scriptural issues can be black and white and difficult to explain. Because we are not God, we might have, for instance, written differently the verse now referenced John 14:6:

Jesus said to him, "I am the way and the truth and the life. No one comes to the Father except through me."

People have written books on this subject, and, let's face it, it's a stickler. I can do little with it in the few remaining pages of this chapter, except to tell you that Jesus said it,

God ordained it, John wrote it, it's *in there!* It's black and white.

It's true.

It may not seem fair. We may not like arguing it or defending it, but it sure sets some parameters for our lives, doesn't it? If any devout, sincere, nice person can get to God in his own way, then the extent of our responsibility to mankind would be to encourage people to be nice. That's easier than telling a Buddhist or a Muslim or a Jew that Jesus is the only way to God.

Amazingly, many devotees of the great religions are unaware of that statement by Jesus. Those who seem nicer and more tolerant than we are will say, "Our faith incorporates yours. We take the truth from all the prophets and holy men. We take the best from Confucius, Buddha, Muhammad, Jesus, and Moses, and we accept all."

What magnanimous people they are! What appealing religion! We're all in this together, they say. Don't be exclusivistic. Don't think you have a monopoly on truth. Let's share the truths and great teachings from all our faiths.

One problem: our Man doesn't fit. He's the one among all the others who says He's the only one. It's right there in black and white. You can't have a harmonious quartet or quintet when one of the members is a self-proclaimed soloist.

When people of other faiths, or people with no faith who "really, really respect what Jesus was all about," find out that He said what He said, they often don't like Him anymore. They consider Him an egotist at best. But as C.S. Lewis wrote, "to make the claim He made, Jesus had to be liar, lunatic, or Lord of all."

People who think the start and finish of the ministry of Jesus came in the Sermon on the Mount need to be gently directed to His more radical statements. When you hear people say, "I think Jesus was a great teacher and prophet, but I don't think he was God or the Son of God," they need to know that He Himself made those claims.

They can't have it both ways. Is a teacher great and wonderful even if he is deluded in thinking he is divine? I had many great teachers in my educational background, limited though it was, but if even my favorite would have said he was the only way to God, I'd have been out of there in a New York minute.

Jesus will not settle for being one of many. He's all there is, the only way to God, and there's no in-between on that. He's living proof of the smaller truth I want you to remember forever: Some things *are* black and white.

Are there exceptions to every rule? Let's jump into abortion and choose up sides right away. You boys know that I came to this fray later than I like to admit, having for years held the milquetoast opinion that "most Christians agree abortion is wrong except in cases of rape and incest or when the life of the mother is at stake . . . blah, blah, blah."

Would you want your twelve-year-old daughter to have to carry a baby conceived in a rape? Should she have to be saddled with adult responsibilities while yet a child herself?

If forced to make a choice between your wife and an unborn infant, would you not choose the life of the mother?

Don't ever, and don't let me ever, be flippant on issues such as these. I say sincerely that I thank God I have never had to make such choices, and I don't want to be glib in saying that the answers would trip so easily off my tongue if I were suddenly thrust into such a situation.

But it has been some years now since I have believed there was an exception to a prohibition against abortion.

The truth came to me fully developed and ready to be believed when Curt Young, then president of the Christian Action Council, said, "If we believe the fetus is an unborn human and that terminating it is the ending of a life, how do we ever justify it?"

But if it is the product of a rape or incest . . .

"It is the innocent party! Just like the victim of the sexual assault, the unborn human is not at fault!"

But why should the girl have to carry a baby to term when she is so young and small and . . . ?

"It's a tragedy, and though carrying a child can be difficult and even traumatic to a young girl's body, if she is old enough to conceive, she should be old enough to carry and deliver it with less trauma than an abortion would inflict upon her."

But she will be reminded every day for nine months of the horrible act perpetrated on her. Can't she just have it aborted and put the crime behind her?

"How does the ending of the life of one of the two innocent parties put anything behind her? If she is party to the abortion, she will live with that horror and trauma."

Should she be expected to raise a child that was forced upon her?

"No, though she may want to when the time comes. But if she does not or doesn't have help, she can place the baby with a loving family."

These issues are not fun, and they are not easy, and I cringe every time I hear someone spout standard answers as if this would not be a gut-wrenching ordeal. But sometimes, I repeat, certain things in life *are* black and white.

What about the "life of the mother" argument? Surely in those cases where you have to chose, it makes sense to chose the mother, doesn't it?

This issue is a stickler even to many who agree with me on the rape and incest question. Dr. C. Everett Koop, for years chief of staff at Philadelphia Children's Hospital, a renowned pediatric surgeon and eventually Surgeon General of the United States, rocked me with a statement in 1976. At a seminar at the Evangelical Press Association convention in Philadelphia, he said that in his *decades* as a pediatric surgeon, he had never once seen or heard of a situation where either the mother's or the unborn baby's life was required to be terminated to save the other.

He wasn't saying it had never happened. He was saying, as probably the world's leading authority in this area, that he was unaware of it. He admitted that yes, in some situations a mother dies in childbirth or an unborn child dies while physicians concentrate on the mother.

But, the question here is whether *abortion* would be justified to save the life of the mother. Perhaps having to neglect the child during a trauma to the mother would cost its life. But is there ever a reason to purposely abort that baby to save the mother? The man who should know says he's never heard of or seen it.

I'm not going to tell you *what* to think. I would be gratified to know that I helped teach you *how* to think. You must make your own decisions in these most earthy and gritty details of life and death. I can't imagine thoughtful Christians coming to other conclusions, but I have to accept that they do, and even that you might. If you study these issues and come down on the other side of them, don't do it because you believe there are no absolutes, no black-and-white answers.

I can lead you only to foundations, like Scripture, and principles—like the fact that although not everything is black and white, some things are. Before God you make decisions to base your life upon. Disagree with me, and I'll love you anyway. I'll never speak to you again, but I'll love you anyway. (Just kidding!)

Do me the favor of remembering that some things *are* black and white.

CULTIVATE
A BEST FRIEND

12

CULTIVATE A BEST FRIEND

I moved away from my best childhood friend twenty-seven years ago. I've visited my hometown a dozen times since then and never run into him. On my most recent trip I talked to his parents, got his California address, and wrote him. It was great to get his letter and reestablish contact.

Ironically, though Dan and I are not related, we share the same last name. We hung around together so much through eighth grade that many assumed we were brothers.

I don't recall meeting Dan for the first time because we were born within a few months of each other and grew

up on the same street. We both had brothers named Jim
Jenkins, virtually the same age. We both had brothers between us and our Jims too. His was Harold. Mine was Jeff.
He had something I didn't have. A little sister. But when
my mother had a ten-years-later tagalong brother, his mother followed suit.

When I first moved away, it was only a block and
didn't affect our friendship. We still did his paper route together. As I recall, Dan was the more openly spiritual of
us. When we talked about paper route arrangements it
was not out of character for him to say he'd pray about it.
It didn't surprise me to hear recently that for a time he was
in the ministry. It's good now to be hearing from him for
the first time since before high school.

There really is no reason we haven't kept in touch
over the years. We used to treat each other's homes like
our own. The Jenkins kids, all of us, played together every
day. We shared a baseball card collection (I won't bore you
with how many tens of thousands it would be worth today).
We endured gym classes and laps and common teachers.

I know nothing of Dan's high school or college careers, his early days in theological studies, his pastorate,
his married life, his children. I know he has five and that a
couple of them have to be older than we were the last time
we saw each other.

The problem is that the miles have done something to
a once best-friendship. We correspond now, and we bring
each other up to date, but it is unlikely we will ever be best
friends again.

We've lost too much of each other. Too much of our
lives will be only news to one while it is made up of mem-
ories for the other.

Dan was an engaging and sensitive fellow. I recall in
sixth grade going with him to the library downtown where
he asked for "anything about God." They gave him a

black suitcase containing what they called "theological rel-ics." He kidded on the bus on the way home that he thought we had some theological relics in our church.

Because of that interest and that sense of humor, I'm assuming Dan has good friends today. I do too. I'm partic-ularly close to three in Illinois. But I also have a best friend. He lives in Michigan. Here's what I wrote about him in my magazine column:

> I'm talking about a guy my age whom I have known since the first week of college. His name is Dave. He is a pastor. We see each other twice, maybe three times a year. With him I can truly be myself. It isn't that I am deceptive with all others, but we do tend to put our best foot forward when relationships are at risk, don't we?
>
> Having to be on our best behavior most of the time isn't all bad. But at times I need to let my hair down, tell somebody *everything*, revert to adolescence, and enjoy a re-lationship built on years of trust and confidence.
>
> Where else—outside my family—can I sing aloud to oldies on the radio, laugh till I cry, recall childish pranks with humor rather than embarrassment, and be myself, warts and all? Dave and I tease that we each have enough knowledge to ruin the other's reputation.
>
> Ours is a friendship that endures, that picks up where it leaves off, even after months of no contact. For some rea-son, busyness I suppose, we hardly ever write or call. We simply live in our own orbits, then debrief each other when the families get together.
>
> Our backgrounds are both different and similar: Dave grew up with sisters, I with brothers, but we were both raised by devout, active evangelicals, quiet, behind-the-scenes type people.
>
> We met the first week at college, hit it off, and talked all night. We've drifted from the others who ran in our crowd more than twenty years ago, but Dave and I are bonded by someone he introduced me to. His girlfriend,

Diane, knew a girl she and Dave thought I should meet. We're still married. Dave and I were in each other's weddings.

Though separated by a couple of hundred miles, Dave and I have been "together" through job changes, moves, disappointments, heartaches, and joys. We turned forty the same fall. I've been gray for fifteen years. He recently started shaving.

When I think of Dave, I'm often reminded of a conversation I had with the crusty, old publisher of the first newspaper I worked for. He once mentioned that he had a twenty-five-year friendship. He must have noticed my blank expression. At barely nineteen I didn't understand the significance.

"How many people do you know," he asked, "who have the same friend that long? Someone who's not related?"

He had a point.

"Someday," he added, "you'll realize how rare it is to have a friend for that long."

Dave and I have seen each other's children grow from infancy to adolescence. I am beginning to see the wisdom of the old publisher's comment.

Dave and I have stood the test of time. We'll make twenty-five years, if God chooses, and it wouldn't surprise me if we were friends as grandparents one day.

I wish I'd known Dave when he was a kid, and I wish I still knew Dan. My challenge to you is to cultivate friendships, ones that will last. When I was playing or delivering papers with Dan Jenkins, there was no past or future. We talked once about maybe going to college together, but that was as far ahead as kids could dream. We didn't try to imagine the other as married, a father, a grandfather.

When Dave and I used to play—instead of studying as we should have—as college students, I knew his girlfriend who became his wife. But I didn't really think ahead to when we would be middle-aged, have seven kids between us, and start thinking about college for them.

Of course, you know Dave's kids. We vacation with them almost every summer. They've been in Brazil for almost a year right now, and I need to write them again. When they get back to their church, we'll see them again. The miles and the months will have had no effect on Dave's and my friendship.

I covet a friendship or two like that for you. I see some developing, and they are ones that could last if you make sure they do.

Best friendships are between people who can be honest with each other, laugh at each other's faults, and don't try to change one another. Best friends are loyal and care and can keep confidences. Best friends can argue and disagree and even raise their voices at each other without worrying an iota about the future of the relationship.

Best friendships are roots. Dave and I know each other's histories from the time we met. I can mention a name or a situation that might take an hour to explain to someone else, and he knows exactly what I'm talking about. We can speak in shorthand in public, making plans and speaking in code about how we need to get going, while the people around us think we're merely gabbing.

We can tell each other things no one else would dare tell us. Bad breath, a runny nose, collar sticking up, shirt-tail hanging out, talking too loud, saying the wrong thing.

"That wasn't really funny."

"Oh, yeah? Drop dead."

"You never have been able to beat me at this game."

"Oh, I am so sure."

Best friends are long past the point of thinking each other has no faults. Knowing each other well and still car-ing about each other is what makes best friends. Best friends aren't made overnight. It takes years.

You guys don't get to have a woman as a best friend, unless it's your wife. Just doesn't work any other way. There's no future in it, no matter what exceptions you hear about or dream about.

And while I am urging you to cultivate a best friend, don't ever let that relationship come between you and your wife. Dave and I are so good about that (could you help pat us on the back? Thanks.) that our wives love to see us get together and run off to play for a while. They are not threatened by our friendship or even the time it sometimes takes. Our friendship is good for our marriages because we admonish and encourage and caution each other. We even have a blood pact. If either of us ever defrauds our marriage partner, the other has promised to beat the tar out of him. I'd do it too, and I know Dave would. No questions asked.

That can never be the only reason to stay maritally pure, but it's an impressive little insurance policy. I think I could take Dave if it was a fair fight, but in that situation we pledged to just drive to the other's state, kick open the front door, and start whalin' away.

I can just hear him saying, "You think you could take me in a fair fight?! C'mon, right now!"

We'd end up at opposite ends of the table tennis table, where I wouldn't have any trouble with him.

"Give me a break! I taught you everything you know."

"Oh, right, serve it up!"

Some friendship, huh? May you have one just like it.

Mom and I want to be your friends too. Always. We won't push. We won't tell you how to run your lives. We'll be proud to see you make your own decisions. We'll be there to help but not to bail you out unless you're desperate. We want to see you learn and grow and develop and mature. As the Gaither song says, we even wish you some losses, because only in losing you win.

Meanwhile we've got a few more years with each of you. We'll drive you crazy half the time, but you'll keep that score even. I'll likely continue to be obnoxious and brag on you all the time.

And I'll keep hammering away on all those thousand and one things a day that I think you should know and remember.

It wasn't easy narrowing this to just twelve things. If there was an over-riding one, one that encompasses this and the myriad others that didn't fit here, you would know exactly what it was. Because for all the mistakes we've made, all the times we've been unnecessarily (and sometimes necessarily) rigid, you need to know that we were just trying to be good parents. We don't have ill motives. We've never done this before.

You think you've never been eight or twelve or fifteen before. Think of us. We've been those ages, but we still lived in caves. And we've never been parents of kids those ages before.

So no matter what you think of rules and regulations and reasons, remember that I'm just trying to be a good dad, I love you, and nothing you can say or do will ever get in the way of that.

EPILOGUE

So can you guys rattle off the twelve things for me? Remember:

Love is not a state of being, it's an act of the will. You shouldn't ever have to ask me if I love your mom. You should see me loving her every day. And I never want to have to ask you if you love your wives. I want to see it proved in how you speak to her, act around her, do for her.

The only goals worth setting are intrinsic and qualitative. If all you worry about is whether you're number one in the universe, you won't even be the best you can be.

We don't quit. Having that somehow drilled into me—mostly by the examples of my parents and my brothers—has born significant fruit in my life. It's not just being stubborn enough to keep looking for something until you find it. It's also persevering, sticking with a request until someone gives you a definite answer. I never would have written *Sweetness* (the Walter Payton biography) if I had grown impatient waiting for word from him or his agent.

Getting a yes and a signature on that contract took nine months (appropriately). I would have taken no for an answer, if that had been what I received. I was simply ignored for months. That can be frustrating and even insulting, but it also taught me a lesson. Those guys and their representatives cannot answer all the people who want something from them. When they become convinced either that someone can benefit them or will not give up until he is answered, then they answer.

That has served me well on all subsequent negotiations with noted personalities. I don't ask them for anything but the time the contract will pay for, and I am not insulted when responses take a long time. That is part of negotiating. The one who needs the relationship least is the one who controls it. When people try to wait you out, never, never, never quit until they say no.

Some people have the right to be wrong. This is one of the hardest and most difficult lessons in life. If I were honest, I'd have to admit my first reaction when people disagree with me is to believe that they are wrong. Isn't that ugly? Of course it is. It's egotistical, self-centered human nature. We all think we're something special, that no one has ever had such insight before. I can run your company better than you can. Why, I could even streamline your mail room. Boss, just let me convince you you're wrong and I'm right on this, and we'll both be happier.

Wrong!

Give your earnest, respectful input, and then trust, support, and even rest in the boss's decision. His becomes yours. He'll know and remember that you were initially cautious about a plan that eventually went wrong. You don't need to remind him, counsel him, scold him. You'd be amazed at the number of people who do that. You've even done it to us. But someone has to be in charge, right or wrong.

There is heavy responsibility and burden on those who must make decisions. They have the right to be wrong. And unless its immoral, unethical, or illegal, do what they say and you'll be far ahead. And someday, you'll be the one with the right to be wrong.

Life isn't fair. Which is proved by the above point. I know people who have sunk into deep depression because life never evened out for them. They were good and kind and noble and honest and true. But unlike in childhood, when that rates you a merit badge, in adulthood you will just as likely, if not more likely, be walked on because you're not just a little dishonest, conniving, maneuvering, manipulating.

I'll be proud to know that my sons do the right thing because it's the right thing and not because they think it'll guarantee any fairness in this cruel world. The Golden Rule is rarely reciprocated, but it's still right. Always.

Take responsibility for your own actions. Even when it is someone else's fault, look for ways, within reason, to protect others from shame, humiliation, embarrassment. And remember that there probably was something you could have done along the way to have precluded the problem. The best delegators I know never blame poor quality or late deliveries on their suppliers. They take full responsibility, even if it means they become a nuisance to those suppliers. Seek responsibility, then take it.

Watch your tongue. I could have written several chapters on how long it took me to learn this lesson. Some people know me as a pretty chatty person, but if they had seen me in high school, they'd think me a monk today. Even sought opinions are rarely appreciated. Do more asking than telling.

Work before you play (delay gratification), but play. The second part of that is easier than the first. Somehow, I think I've been a wonderful example to you in getting in a lot of play time. I can only hope and pray that you were aware that I paid my dues to be able to play.

In fact, the way I was raised—even though my brothers would remember me as "the lazy one"—I got the message. My Protestant work ethic makes me feel guilty when I'm not working, so I have to pay in advance with lots of production. Then I can relax and enjoy.

Women work harder than men. I know, I know. Saying that aloud will get you into as much trouble as it will likely get me for putting it on paper. You already know you wouldn't want to be saddled with the physical trauma of giving birth and its attendant miseries. But the work women do that is harder than men only begins with childbirth. Never forget that. It'll make you a better husband and more sensitive father. (And unlike my father and me, you may even have a daughter or two.)

Play to your strengths. I'm thrilled that you all have many. Don't ignore weaknesses in areas that must be bolstered, but don't waste your life trying to be a professional athlete if your strength is really in music. And vice-versa.

Some things are black and white. Especially John 14:6. Knowing that has carried the day for me in many otherwise wishy-washy situations. It's hard enough to be sure of anything in this relativistic age. Love your relatives, but don't let the relativists play with your mind.

Cultivate at least one life-long friend. The media pretends that such relationships are common. Ask around. You'll discover they're rare. And priceless. Start early, because they take all the time you'll give them. Sometimes you'll find your best friend is your best source of accountability. The man without accountability is headed for disaster. I want you to head for life more abundant.

The day will come, I pray, when you think of the following Scriptures as you think of your best friend. If we could have this attitude toward each other as well, I would consider it a crowning achievement as a dad.

> I thank my God upon every remembrance of you, always in every prayer of mine making request for you all with joy, for your fellowship in the gospel from the first day until now, being confident of this very thing, that He who has begun a good work in you will complete it until the day of Jesus Christ . . . how greatly I long for you all with the affection of Jesus Christ. And this I pray, that your love may abound still more and more in knowledge and all discernment, that you may approve the things that are excellent, that you may be sincere and without offense till the day of Christ, being filled with the fruits of righteousness which are by Jesus Christ, to the glory and praise of God. (Philippians 1:3-6, 8-11)

Moody Press, a ministry of the Moody Bible Institute,
is designed for education, evangelization, and edification.
If we may assist you in knowing more about Christ
and the Christian life, please write us without obligation:
Moody Press, c/o MLM, Chicago, Illinois 60610.